VISIBLE

VISIBLE

Learn to leverage the online
world with no bullshit, so you
stop struggling and start getting
a return on your investment

NICOLA MORAS

First published in 2018
by Covert Marketing
PO Box 10227 Mildura
VIC, 3502

nicolamoras.com.au

Cover design by Ellie Schroeder
ellieschroeder.com

ISBN: 978-1-925846-30-0
Published by Vivid Publishing
A division of Fontaine Publishing Group
P.O. Box 948, Fremantle
Western Australia 6959
www.vividpublishing.com.au

NATIONAL LIBRARY OF AUSTRALIA

A catalogue record for this book is available from the National Library of Australia

This book is dedicated to you: the entrepreneurs, change makers, thought leaders, business owners and organisations who are out there helping make the world a better place.

My wish is that this book helps you to help more people.

PRAISE FOR NICOLA'S WORK

Thank goodness for Nicola Moras's book! If you want to use social media and the digital space to build your brand then look no further. Nicola's no-nonsense approach backed up with evidence-based results will help you develop the digital plan you need to support your success.

Janine Garner

I've been working with Nicola and all I can say is WOW!

I wanted to take my coaching and mentoring business from being completely reliant on offline marketing (networking, referrals, etc.) and learn how to use online marketing (particularly Facebook ads).

Within the first three weeks, Nicola had taught me how to design my entire marketing program, write my Facebook ads, create my landing pages, and in that time, I started generating leads from my Facebook ads! On average, I was getting two to seven new leads each day, and they were the exact types of clients I was looking to work with.

By week eight or nine, I had to turn off my Facebook ads because I was getting too many leads! I couldn't believe it! What a great problem to have!

Ellen Bathgate, RentRoll Starter

Nicola doesn't hold back, there's no sugar coating of the truth and it was just the kick I needed to start to do things differently, with a big improvement in engagement in just the first week.

Dr Jenny Brockis

We had been in business four years before we met Nicola. Limping along trying to build the business up with very little money for marketing, going nowhere fast. We had tried traditional methods of marketing with little or no success. We were lost and had no idea what to do next. It was looking like our business was about to fail.

What Nicola taught us in the first few months turned our mindset around and we made more in the first three months than we had made in the previous year.

Jeromy Baird & Kim Fullager

Before working with Nicola I had no idea where to start when it came to marketing myself and my business. I was overwhelmed with the amount of information out there and honestly, just wanted someone to tell me the steps that I needed to take – as well as teach me how to make it all work together.

Nicola not only knows her marketing shiz – she knows people. I am excited to grow my business. Marketing can be tricky but it's completely understandable and logical now that I know how the process works.

Kelly Drobek

The best part about working with Nicola is her ability to see what you need to work on to drive and create results. She's a marketing genius and together with her knowledge on business, she's the best person to show you how to do it.

Nicola is the real deal. You will never regret investing in yourself and your business! Thank you for the privilege of working with you!

Susie Gasparovic

ABOUT THE AUTHOR

Nicola Moras is passionate about helping business owners and companies generate results from social media and digital marketing, without the bullshit. This means actually getting a financial return on investment.

With a 12-year career in financial services as her foundation to creating a powerful personal brand, she decided to launch her own business helping others to market themselves with an online focus. Why? Because she wanted to help people in a more powerful way to achieve their goals of financial freedom and joy in their lives.

Nicola has helped thousands of people and companies around the world with their social media and digital marketing strategies. By creating visibility, impact and profits, she has helped these clients become 'professionally famous' online.

She has been vlogging regularly since 2011 and guest blogging for Arianna Huffington's Thrive Global (media and tech company) since 2016. She has been featured in *Huffington Post*, *Influencive*, *Working Women Magazine*, *Bossbabe*, and *GLOSS* magazine and has worked with Telstra, MADEC Australia, Fishers Supermarkets and numerous city councils. She is regularly invited to speak to networking groups and organisations.

Nicola lives in 'the middle of nowhere' in a regional town called Mildura – the food bowl of Australia. In her spare time she raises her three children, hangs out with her husband, Dominic, and plays (and trains for!) roller derby. Why roller derby? Because you have to concentrate completely on what you're doing, otherwise you land on your backside!

She wholeheartedly believes that you are your best and most important asset and that you should become omnipresent on social media and through your digital marketing efforts – with the view to be getting results. She believes in the power of you.

Contents

FOREWORD

We are living in a very exciting time. It is easier than ever before for a solopreneur or an entrepreneur to launch a business without a brick-and-mortar store front, and even to do business online from a beach in Belize while the money continues to pour in 24 hours a day from our online efforts that can continue to drive revenue even while we sleep.

This vast new landscape of opportunity and possibility, which was largely responsible for the $100 million in sales that I was blessed to do of my own seminars and training over the years, also provides us with some unique challenges.

There's a cacophony of voices telling us what to do in order to grow our businesses and to put the scaffolding underneath our every dream. Sorting through all of these voices and knowing who to listen to in order to lay out the best roadmap to win the game can be beyond challenging. What's needed, more so perhaps than ever before, is a guided approach to business building that takes in mind the full picture of what the entrepreneur is looking to accomplish and strategies that are reverse-engineered from the perspective of the individual goals of the business owner.

For example, if you were to build a house you wouldn't start by making the decision to build the house, and then put in place a kitchen sink and a toilet. Instead you would find an architect who has built many houses of the type you are looking to build, and then you would work with that architect to put together the plans for the house before working to implement those plans.

Nicola Moras is much like the master architect from the perspective of having the experience and insight and ability to help you reverse engineer your dream and to put in place the plan to provide for a solid foundation of serious growth and monetisation.

I still remember my first ever telephone conversation with Nicola: I became so curious about her business, as it was very clear that Nicola, of the thousands of business owners I speak to, was someone who was actually really working systems and had the money coming in hand over fist. I remember how impressed I was with Nicola and what she was doing that I made a conscious decision to keep an eye on her progress. It was obvious that she was someone who would continue to grow and to produce phenomenal results.

What was it about her that made her stand out? It's a good question. It's been said that dreams are a dime a dozen but it's execution that produces results.

Nicola was executing and continues to do so at high levels.

This level of execution oftentimes just comprises simple things done consistently over time, which lead to enormous success.

When Nicola asked me to write the foreword for the book – I said yes to do something that virtually never occurs in my world. I, like everyone else, have a very busy calendar but this was different. I was so impressed with who Nicola was that I was clear that I wanted to write the foreword and I even thought this is MY opportunity that will be missed if I don't say yes!

In reading Nicola's work I have only become more clear about the desire to be a part of her project, primarily to help YOU get YOUR hands on this powerful information and the strategies that Nicola shares.

We need experienced voices and guides who we can count on to deliver the goods and I can tell you that you've come to the right place with Nicola.

The landscape of social media has been rapidly growing and evolving, and navigating the playing field can be full of challenges, pitfalls and sand traps that can threaten to turn the whole experience into a downward spiral into the abyss of wasted time and money.

For a business owner the discussion used to be about whether to do social media or not. But then somewhere between 2010 and 2015 it became brutally obvious that if you weren't involved in social media you were going to fall behind. Within that same time frame the results that we used to get with email marketing were now coming from social media. With the decreasing open rates of email, combined with social media marketing hitting its stride, there became no way to stay out of it.

But as Nicola clearly points out in this book, social media can either be a bottomless pit for money with the necessity of social media managers who often have 'institutional branding' as the goal, rather than actual direct response marketing, which is infinitely more measurable.

What impresses me most about Nicola's viewpoints on this is the fact that she knows the direct response game and how to monetise social media fast. She also knows the importance of institutional branding and the long game. And she adeptly uses her vast experience in both of these areas to help YOU create a social media architecture for your business and your life.

Without the short game of immediate and measurable monetisation of social media efforts combined with long-term institutional branding woven into the marketing efforts a business may never get off the ground, and all sorts of people's dreams may be shattered on the rocks of poor strategy, planning and implementation.

I'm also impressed by Nicola's integrity and heart, which have only become more and more clear to me over the years of knowing her.

With Nicola on your team and by your side I have no doubt but that you have a very powerful guide who will help you navigate the social media playing field to achieve your greatest dreams.

Nicola's methodology and strategies provide you with a pathway to the implementation of social media strategies that provide clarity and a lantern in the dark on the path toward multiplying your revenue and building a powerful brand in the age of 'Brand You'.

It's been said that the journey of a thousand miles begins with a single step, but if you get stuck on the first step that's a problem, so dive in, proceed with abandon, know that you're in the right hands, and someday please find me and share with me all of your successes!

Until then...

Love deeply, shine brightly and make everyday an extraordinary adventure!

Chris Howard
Best-selling author and transformational wealth coach

INTRODUCTION

Your alarm goes off in the morning and while you're lying in bed thinking about how your day is going to pan out, you decide that TODAY is the day.

You open your phone and check Facebook and LinkedIn. You have a quick look at Instagram and your emails – just to get a pulse on what's going on out there in the world. With a burst of energy, you leap out of bed and start getting ready for the day ahead.

While you're in the shower you come up with all sorts of ideas of what you can share and how you can share it. Isn't it funny how water can have that kind of effect on your creative brain? You get yourself sorted, head to the office and open up your computer. Coffee in hand, of course! You open a social media account and flick through the newsfeed again thinking to yourself 'I *know* I need to post something' and you open your own profile (or business page) and you're greeted by that blank space where you need to start typing.

This is exactly when that familiar overwhelmed feeling kicks in. It's like opening up a word document knowing that you need to start writing but you're being stared down by the flashing cursor on the screen. #unhelpful!

For me, this feels like the time that I missed my cue in a high-school stage production. The whole theatre was silent except for the whispers of prompts coming from my fellow cast members. An eternity passed before I realised that they were for me. UGH. I'll never forget that feeling of stage fright combined with red-faced sheer embarrassment. My stomach lurched into my throat and I felt sick. I felt like I had let everyone down.

It doesn't feel good letting people down when you've made the commitment to showing up. This is how many people feel when it comes to social media. Like they're missing their cue.

You've probably picked up this book because you know that your online presence isn't doing what it should be doing. It's not producing results and you're probably not making money from it. So something needs to change.

I know that everyone is so damn busy that to find the time to do this online work can feel like a constant hustle. It's tiring just thinking about how to fit this extra thing we 'have to do' into our to-do lists.

This is why many people chose to outsource their social media activity. I'm talking about the posting, the creative and even the writing. They hire a public relations person or a virtual assistant to promote them. But is it working? Virtual assistants can create pretty posts, talk branding and colour palettes and getting at least one post up per day so you're seen as consistent, but are they getting return on investment? No. Can they measure it? No.

I am so tired of seeing people like you spend ridiculous amounts of money outsourcing this work, hiring social media managers and PR agents who:

1. Can't or won't share what's working or why it's not working

2. Don't know *how* to measure the actual results

3. Take your money but don't reply to emails or can't provide a report

4. Take months to get anything up and running and can't explain why; or blame *you* for not providing them with what they needed in order to get it up and running

Most of all, though, I'm tired of you being taken advantage of.

On the other hand, I've met many of you struggling to do it all on your own. You've done your best. You've followed the lists. You've ticked the boxes. You've been working through what you feel like you should be doing, posting everywhere because you've been told you have to ... and you probably haven't even seen any results for it.

My commitment to you is this:

This book is going to be the bridge from knowing you *should* be online to knowing *why* you need to be online and *what* you need to do make this happen.

My mission — both through this book and all the other work that I'm doing — is to show you how you can use these amazing platforms for results, not just ticking the boxes while hoping for something magical to happen.

So here's what we're going to do. (I heard the sigh of relief! You're in good hands.)

First, I'm going to convince you that *you* need to take ownership for this. You cannot outsource your social media if you really want to get results.

Next, we're going to agree that you do need to get a return on investment from this thing called 'social'. However, we're going to shift away from using that as the sole focal point, and make sure that we're approaching the Land of Online with the intention of using it as a tool to build relationships — without you needing to be 'in the room' or 'in person' doing all of the time-consuming 1:1 work.

I know that most people get 'analysis paralysis' when they try to work out what to post and where to post it. There are so many choices with platforms and content delivery. Should you video or should you write? Do you post memes or should you share other people's posts? I know they also worry about when to post. Do you have to schedule posts or do you have to be live when you're posting?

Then there's the question of how much volume to post, and the fear of failure I see in everyone from start-ups to seasoned professionals.

Don't worry; I've got your back. We are going to cover all this.

Please note that this book is not a social media management plan; it's a strategy about everything you do online, from your website, to your social media profiles, to your email lists.

So let's level with each other before we crack into it with some truth bombs:

- Saying your people aren't on Facebook or social media is an excuse and you need to stop saying it.

- Saying 'everyone is jumping off Facebook' is catastrophising and ridiculous. Also, it's an excuse that's holding you back from actually getting yourself out there.

- You can't just throw money at something and expect that it's going to work. You're smart. You know this.

- If you don't have a strategy, no social media or online platform will work.

- Algorithms change all the time. You, however, can have control over your message, your positioning and your strategy.

- The ROI process has not changed at all since I started using Facebook for business in 2010 and started paying for advertising in 2011. It's the exact same relationship-building, (direct response marketing) process that has been used for years. Sometimes the tactical implementation may differ, and this is where social media managers come unstuck, because they don't necessarily understand the overall strategy of what you're trying to achieve.

- People on LinkedIn will scoff at Facebook and people on Facebook scoff at LinkedIn. Let's just stop it and use these platforms that we have available to us and stop with the schoolyard bullying!

- Each platform has a distinct purpose and way to use it. Determining where your audience is will help with the choice.

Are you ready to get started?

Awesome! Let's go.

PART ONE

CHANGE
YOUR
APPROACH

THERE ARE MANY THINGS THAT people don't really like doing, like ironing or cleaning or cooking or adulting! Yes, some of things on that list that can be outsourced, but you cannot outsource your social media if you want to be visible.

Marketing is all about getting people to know you, like you and trust you, right? Yes! (Glad you're with me here.) So if you're not showing up, if it's not you who is showing up, then your audience is going to be liking and trusting someone else.

It's a bit like sitting on the bench, knowing that you can play the game awesomely but constantly being overlooked because you're afraid to put your hand up, to say 'Hey! I'm here and I'm ready!'

Truly, it's time to get in the game. To be seen for who you are and how you can help your audience.

We have a brilliant problem right now in the world of social media that you can use to your advantage. This problem is that everyone is outsourcing the majority of what they're putting out there, which contributes to the bigger problem of everyone looking the same and sounding the same. Everyone is looking for a way to stand out, but they're all doing the same things! The great news is that you have everything you need at your fingertips to be able to stand out from the pack. To be visible.

The added benefit is that you can use this to control the conversation that your audience is having in their heads about you and what it is that you 'do'.

Buuuut let's not get ahead of ourselves. First we've got to bring it back to foundation level, and that foundation is all about building relationships online.

And much like dating, building relationships requires you! You being there, you being part of the conversation and you showing up.

Time to get off the bench!

1

THE DATING GAME

I WANT YOU TO PUT YOURSELF in the very fabulous shoes of a single woman and you've gone to a local bar with a group of friends – the one where you've been told all the quality people hang out. After all, you're selective about who you'd like to let into your life. You're ready to have a great night out.

The music is on. You've been dancing and now you're parched, so you head to the bar. A guy you don't know, but were admiring from across the room, comes over and offers to buy you a drink. You say 'Yes, thanks! That would be lovely' and you accept the drink. (Although it may have been more like 'Ooh yes!' with a sparkle in the eye). The barman hands the drink over and you make sure you take it straight from his hand because a) you're safety conscious and b) the bar is sticky! (ew).

You turn to the guy who bought you the drink and say, 'Thanks so much. I'd like to introduce you to Pattie, my assistant. I'm so super busy so she's going to take care of getting to know you. Then we can organise to catch up again later if we decide to.' And without another word, you twirl back towards the dance floor where your friends are standing with their jaws dropping to the floor. Your assistant Pattie was more than ready to cozy up with your prospective boyfriend, under the guise of 'doing the research for you'.

Could you imagine! You may as well have thrown a glass of cold water all over the poor guy! Pattie wasn't too phased, though, particularly because she thought he was cute, too.

Or what about this one?

The guy you were admiring comes over and offers to buy you a drink, which you accept. You have this great connection, awesome conversation and decide to exchange phone numbers. You agree that you'll catch up for coffee over the next couple of days, but your schedule blows up!

In this scenario, you again send Pattie (your trusty wing woman) to alleviate some of the scheduling pressure and she reports back that the guy is amazing. You organise another date, but again, your schedule blows out, so Pattie is off again!

Your assistant reports that she is making some serious headway with the guy and you realise that you really need to show up to this next date, or you need to just let him go. But, you find out upon chatting with him, that he's actually really hit it off with Pattie and is no longer interested in you because you didn't bother to turn up to the dates!

Oh no. You just lost out on building a potential relationship with someone.

You can't outsource romance. And you can't outsource relationship building either. It has to be you.

My approach to marketing and social media is the same. It's all about relationship building. People won't want to connect with the 'cardboard cutout' version of you that tends to be created by outsourcing. To build a relationship with someone, you need to show up! It has to be you who builds the connection. People need to get to know you in order to determine if they like you or not.

In my humble opinion, there are some things you simply cannot outsource:

- Social media
- Dating
- Video blogging
- Sex with your partner
- Yoga
- Sleep
- Catching up with family and your friends

(This list is not an exhaustive list, obviously! But you get the point!)

It's got to be you

Your personal brand is the sum total of what you do, how you do it and why you do it. It's not something you can fake. It's authentic and deep-seated.

Clement Lim, *Entrepreneur Magazine*

Everyone is looking for a way to stand out and be different. They want to be relevant and to create connection. If you're an entrepreneur, an intrapreneur or even a CEO the time is now to start building your personal brand online and strategically using social media to do this.

As Jeff Bezos (founder of Amazon) famously said, 'Your brand is what people say about you when you're not in the room'.

With the amount of noise that is going on out there online, which isn't showing any signs of letting up any time soon, the time truly is now for you to start to increase the quantity and quality of what you are putting out into the online world in the form of content and value. Essentially, you are marketing *you* out there. It's the same as you heading out on a Saturday night looking amazing in your favourite going-out outfit, hair just right, feeling like you're being the best version of yourself. Treat social media that way and things will shift.

The competition is fierce in the digital world. Just like being overlooked when you're sitting on the bench or glanced over and ignored while standing at the bar waiting to order a drink, there are more and more people coming up all the time. It's the way you show up that will help you to stand out.

You cannot afford to get swallowed up in the crowd because you look or sound the same as everyone else. Not when you have a business and a profile to build.

There are the youngsters who are doing this without any effort. They've been on social media from a very young age, whereas for us 'older folk' (anyone over the age of 25!) it's not as natural for us. It's not part of our DNA: it's something that needs to be learned. And because we're so caught up in trying to do it 'right' and tick the boxes, we can lose ourselves along the way.

The vital thing to understand about building your brand is that marketing is all about invoking the 'know you, like you and trust you' feeling around everything that you're doing. And the only way that to do that is by being authentically you.

It's critical that everything you put out into the online world (and offline for that matter) lets people get to *know you* as someone who cares and who is genuine. This will help them *like you*. When you are consistently showing up, sharing yourself and your knowledge genuinely, they will come to *trust you*.

Trust can be slow to build and fast to lose. In order for someone to trust you, they need to see a consistent version of you everywhere they come across you. Your voice needs to be the same, your message needs to be the same, your tone needs to be the same. Most of all, you need to show that you walk your talk – which means you're living and breathing the philosophies that you're sharing. If not, you risk creating distrust.

For example, if you're a health coach or a nutritionist and you're advocating for healthy lifestyles and good food choices yet you are out on the weekend eating fast food, drinking sugary drinks and lots of alcohol and smoking, this is going to create a profound disconnect of trust and rapport.

It takes time

Trust is built over time and you are not in control of that timeline. Some people trust quickly, while others need more time. This is why it's imperative to learn how to use social media, digital platforms and your websites to play both the long game and the short game. This means leveraging what is being put out there right now in order to connect with your audience as well as building long-term relationships with them. This helps to build both consistency and trust.

The short game

This is about connecting with the people who are quicker to trust. For example, someone sees what you've been posting and 'stalks' you for a while. They have a look at your website, they suss you out, then decide relatively quickly that they need your help. This can happen over a period of hours or a few days.

The short game is great for those in your audience who are already 'sold' on you and what you're putting out there. They're generally the ones who need fewer interactions and touch points with you in order for them to feel confident to make buying decisions.

Example: I recently saw a post on Facebook advertising sleep-in hair curlers made of memory foam. I was impressed with the video. I read the testimonials. I went to the website and checked them out to make sure I could pay using PayPal because #internetsecurity! Feeling satisfied that I could trust that website and that they could deliver on the product, I purchased. This is the short game in action. They had my money within the space of about 15 minutes!

The long game

This is where you need to commit to being present for the long haul when marketing yourself. It means building up content and your profile over an extended period of time to build relationships with your audience.

For example, someone finds you online, decides to follow you, look at your posts, read your blogs or watch your video blogs (vlogs), but doesn't take action to get some help from you at that particular time. They keep following you and watching what you put up. Then, one day – perhaps two months or two years later (or even five in the case of a client of mine) they decide to buy from you. You have built up their trust and they're in. They're loyal and they're so ready for you.

Example: I started following a mentor of mine in 2010. I'd had various mentors throughout my business journey, yet I was still watching her online and receiving her emails. It wasn't until 2017 that I decided that the time was right to work with her given where I was at. I'd followed for seven years before I handed over one red cent. I got to know her early on. I learned to like her over the years. I trusted her before making the decision to buy from her and then she extended an invitation to become a client, which I accepted. That is the long game in action.

I have found over the past eight years that 75% of people that I have spoken with have needed between seven and ten touch points with an individual or a company before they'll make a buying decision. These touch points can be in the form of reading posts, speaking with you personally, attending events and even just watching your vlogs. Their buying decision may be a financial buying decision or it may be the 'I buy into your philosophy' decision. We'll be going into more detail about this later.

Seven to ten touch points is a lot, which is why it's a long game. The good news is that you can play both games concurrently so long as you're consistent across both.

We need to be honest with each other. And that means sharing some home truths with you.

TRUTH BOMB #1: This isn't an overnight fix, which is why you need to commit to playing both the short game and the long game.

TRUTH BOMB #2: It's going to take time, consistency and energy. Much like a steam train that's sitting cold in the station waiting for someone to stoke the fire.

TRUTH BOMB #3: It won't happen overnight, but it will happen if you commit.

Are you with me? Outstanding.

The five phases of relationship building

We build relationships bit by bit, over time. If you want to build a new friendship, you don't go from not knowing someone to suddenly sharing all of your deepest secrets and thoughts with them. It takes time and incremental additions to the friendship to build trust and rapport.

Stephen R Covey talks about this in his book *The 7 Habits of Highly Effective People*. He calls it the 'trust account' strategy. To paraphrase for you, for every positive interaction with someone you gain one point, and you keep gaining points for every positive interaction. This adds 'trust widgets' into your trust account with that person.

When it comes to relationship building on social media, similar thinking is necessary. We need to add value to our audience multiple times in order to gain and *retain* their trust and attention. I call this 'value stacking' (more on this later).

Building relationships and trust online is similar to what you would do offline while attending networking events, dinners or even seminars. Imagine you attend a networking event filled with people you have never met before. I suspect that you would focus on interacting with a few people. You'd start by asking them some questions and they'd answer them. Then they would ask you some questions and you'd answer them. This goes back and forth for a while and you start to form an opinion about that person. You decide if you 'gel' with them and if they are someone you might want to have further conversations with or get to know better. (Or not!) You might decide to exchange contact details and connect after the event.

Let's be honest. You probably wouldn't want to have lunch with someone who you don't get along with, so you need to find a way to determine if they're someone that you want to spend time with. This is where the question and answer conversations become super important.

When we're online, we don't have time to interact with every single person we come into contact with individually like this, but time is on our side in another way because we can build trust and rapport by being consistent over time with what we post online.

This illustration shows the five progressive phases of developing online relationships, which centres on the 'know you, like you, trust you' feeling that is essential to building relationships online.

1. I DON'T KNOW YOU

They don't know you as you and you're not sharing anything much at all

3. LIKE YOU

They start to like you through the high-value content you are offering

5. BUY FROM YOU

Another satisfied customer!

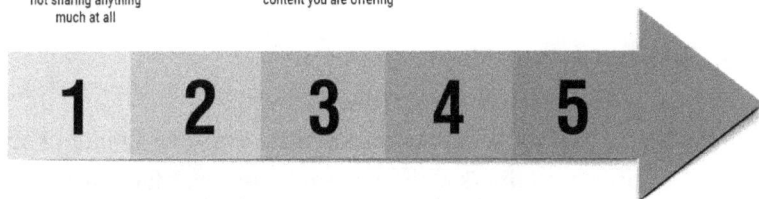

1 2 3 4 5

2. KNOW YOU

They get to know you through what you post and share

4. TRUST YOU

They believe in you and the value of the content you are sharing

Let's break down the phases.

1. Don't know you

This is when you're not really online at all. You may have a Facebook business page but you haven't posted any content on it, or perhaps you have a website but there's just the mandatory 'home' and 'about' pages. There is no other content for your audience to engage with.

You may be posting quotes now and again but it's very random. When people go and look at what you've put out there, they get the feeling that it's sporadic and a bit slap-dash. This stops trust and rapport-building dead in its tracks.

You've got to be posting more so that you can move your audience through to getting to know you.

2. Know you

You're posting every now and again on Facebook or another platform. You may be blogging intermittently. You could even be putting out some free content by way of downloads or checklists.

You may be posting a quote and sharing a blog you've written or filmed. You made the decision to be a bit more active and it's paying off, because it's enough for your audience to learn more about who you are as person based on what you're putting out.

They feel like they're getting to know you.

Example: A bakery posts photos of their cupcake creations and photos of happy customers with huge smiles on their faces when they come in to collect their orders. They might even share a nice post from someone else that resonates with their mindset or values. Their audience then feels safe because they may share similar values and views of the world.

3. Like you

Your audience – the people following you – are really starting to like you because it's you who is showing up (thank goodness!) You're resonating with them and they are getting some value from your content. There's a value–message match happening at this point in time.

Your audience at this point feels like they really like you. They resonate with the content you're putting up there. They see elements of your personality shining through with what you're putting out online and they like what you're about.

Example: A personal trainer posts content on his page regularly, and because some of the issues his clients deal with relate to food and mindset, he decides to include free content on how to manage mindset and how to make good food choices. He starts building up his profile as an expert by sharing content that solves problems his audience has. This is a value-message match.

A value-message match is what occurs when you are posting content that is of value, which also ties into the message that you're putting out there.

4. Trust you

Your audience knows you and likes you, they have probably 'internet stalked' you a bit to check out what you've put up online, and now they trust you. They trust that you're reputable and that you know what you're talking about. You have contributed in some way to their day or their life, and they feel that they can get even more value by working with you at this point. They want your help.

You may think that your job is done when you reach this point, but you're not done yet. We've got to get your audience through to the final phase, which is where a financial exchange takes place. They buy a product or a service from you.

They do this because you've been sharing so much in the form of content, images and added value that they believe in you. They trust in what you have to say.

5. Buy from you

It's in the transition from 'trust you' to 'buy from you' that you start asking people to commit in some way to working with you, either by purchasing some kind of product from you or learning from you.

But, remember, you can't do it on your timeline. It's got to be on theirs. Some people will get to this phase really quickly, while others may take years. I've had people follow me for five years before buying from me and others have purchased seriously high-end program within hours of finding me. This is the long game and the short game in action. And this is where consistency is king.

The long and the short of it

Let me introduce you to Cait, a multi-modality therapist who started following me in 2011. Yes, 2011! She was following me for years – watching my posts, following my blogs, reading my emails and watching what I was doing. She did not interact visibly with me on any platform, though. I did not notice her name pop up anywhere. Then, in 2017 she attended a free training session I was running on marketing and decided that day that she needed to work with me. This is an example of me playing the long game in my business.

By comparison, Kelly-Ann started following me on a Thursday in 2015. She found me by way of a Facebook advert. She applied to have a conversation with one of my team, which we scheduled for later that day. The very next day, she enrolled in my high-level 12-month mastermind program. She told me on the phone that when she found me she went through all of my posts, read everything and looked at my website, and felt like I was the right person to work with. This is an example of a short game in my business.

From invisible to visible

When you really embrace this social relationship-building way of life, you'll find that you go from being invisible to being visible to your audience.

When you're invisible online it's disheartening. It can feel like you're the world's best-kept secret. You've been doing all of this work, putting in the effort, but it's a bit like singing opera in the shower – if no one hears you, can you really sing?

Feeling like you're invisible online can also impact your confidence – particularly if you're like me and love the external validation that what you're doing is great. There's nothing quite as dispiriting as putting your best stuff out into the world and not getting a single reaction. #crickets

Let's not do that for any longer than is necessary.

So what's the next step up from that? It's being visible. Being seen. Being recognised as someone who has something of value and substance to share, which is great, because here's what I know to be true: there is not one other human on the planet like you. There is not one other human who has your knowledge, your experience and your stories, and it's these that make you *you*, and it's these that are going to help you to stand out and be seen.

It's in the nuances of *your* stories that help cement this relationship building process online. This is what makes you different – even if you were standing next to someone who was your identical twin from a knowledge and experience perspective. There are going to be things about you that resonate with your ideal audience that wouldn't resonate with theirs. (We're going to work on this in Chapter 5).

For example, there are thousands of business coaches and marketers out there, but none have lived my life. Nobody else has worked with my clients in the way that I have. I've had many successes and many failures, wins and losses. I've battled through what I have and in my own way. Not one other person on this planet has grown the way that I have, because not a single other person has lived my life.

Leveraging your unique personality and experiences holds a lot of power in social media marketing.

It's you that your prospective clients are hungry to get to know.

There's nobody else out there quite like you. You rock star, you.

Now that we know that this is where the power is, you can start to use this when it comes to building your visibility.

What happens when you're visible? This is where the financial return on investment kicks in. This is where you start being recommended to other people because of what you're putting up online. Referrals happen. Recommendations start to flow.

This is where you start to get approached for speaking engagements. This is where you influence your audience. This is when you generate more sales into your programs or products. This is where you become the employee of choice, the reason why your new employer should hire you versus a different person.

The ROI is huge when you're using the online world to become visible.

Where are the gaps?

Remember that the way to build relationships online is not really very different to the way you build them in person.

To start, find a common link with the person (your audience), much like you would if you were meeting someone for the first time. This requires you to ask questions and really listen to the things that your audience is telling you in terms of the problems that you're going to be solving.

Take a look at how you're currently building relationships online. Are you doing things in such a way that what you're putting out there takes your audience on a relationship journey with you? If not, how can you adjust that? And if you are, brilliant! How can you do more of that?

For example, most people think online marketing is just saying 'Buy my stuff!' They put up some mediocre posts in the hope that people will see value and give them money for their latest product or service. But there's no relationship building going on there.

Now you can see clearly how you're doing it offline and how you're doing it online: where are the gaps?

2

PERFECTLY IMPERFECT

EVERY CLIENT I WORK WITH tells me that they worry about putting themselves out there online. They worry about how they're going to be perceived, how they're going to position themselves and every one of them worries about what it is that they're going to post. They believe that they need to have everything perfect before getting themselves out there.

Ahh, perfectionism. You'll be very happy to hear that being imperfect is actually going to help you to build trust online. More on that later. Let's first take a look at what you have to offer.

I remember the day clearly when I walked into my very first networking event outside of my home town. Up to that point I had been doing most of my marketing online, but I felt like I lacked the in-person contact that I know I thrive upon.

The event was in the city and I was so nervous. The morning before the session I was stressing over what I was going to wear, how I was going to introduce myself and the kind of impression I was going to make. I was still 'hung over' from my corporate job, believing that in order to be taken seriously I needed to be 'professional'. To me, being professional meant being prim and proper, with my suit perfectly tailored. But I was more interested in coming across as someone who was different, who was approachable and friendly as well as professional, and I was worried about how I was going to achieve that balance. This was 2010 and I was still early enough in my journey that I was looking for some of that external approval from people who I thought would become peers of mine.

I decided on a dress with blue and white horizontal stripes on the skirt and a white shirt-like top. Think of a 50s dress – small waist and big full skirt. I felt like a million dollars. And when I walked into the room, OH. MY. GOSH! I was surrounded by women who were wearing pantsuits or very office-y dresses. They were dressed in a very corporate way. They looked great, but I stood out! I walked in feigning confidence and *hoping* that I would be taken seriously by all the business types. Conversely, I also wanted to make sure that I was being 'me' and I hoped that people would like me for how I was, even if I didn't fit the 'professional' model.

It worked!

I had some great conversations and I laughed a lot – which is something that is important to me. I made some great connections, and later people said that they remembered who I was in large part due to how I was dressed and the impression I made when I walked in. #winning! They told me that they appreciated my high energy, smiles and enthusiastic conversation.

Thinking back to our dating analogy, you need to do something similar if you want to stand out, right? If you turn up wearing the same thing as everyone else, trying to fit in because you're afraid of rejection, but hoping to stand out at the same time, well, you're probably not going to get very far.

You need to be able to stand out first and foremost because you need to catch the attention of your audience, and you can do this with the way that you present yourself online. And the best way to present yourself online is to be 100% you. Because you, my friend, are one in a bazillion. You're unique. You're amazing.

So let's get you from feeling exposed yet invisible to feeling confident to put yourself out there as you.

You have to stop hiding. Like, right now

People have all sorts of reasons for why they haven't increased their presence online. Some of them may be valid and some ... well ... not so much! I'm sure some people had to wash the cat rather than doing the Facebook Live or filming the vlog!
One reason I hear a lot is 'my people are not on Facebook' (or LinkedIn, or Instagram or [insert platform of choice]). This is probably not one of your excuses or you wouldn't be reading this book. But just in case you have doubts, let me throw a few stats at you.

- Facebook alone at the time of writing has 2.2 billion users and 1.1 billion daily active users, and users spend on average 40 minutes per day on the platform.

- Instagram has 500 million daily active users and they spend on average 20 minutes per day on the platform.

- LinkedIn has 250 million daily active users and they spend on average 10 minutes per day on the platform.

In the past we have not seen anything like this. Our audiences are actively hanging out more than ever in one easy-to-access place. This is why social media is such a powerful place to start building the 'know you, like you, trust you' process.

You can rest assured that the audience that you want to get in front of is online. They are probably not on most of these platforms to do business; they are on there hanging out. They are killing time, checking up on what their children, parents and friends are doing.

It's the ultimate reality channel for you to connect with people when their attention is not on what's going on around them, but rather what's happening on their phones or computers. The other benefit of this is that people are a lot more open and receptive to marketing when they are relaxed, which is how most people are when they are on social media.

Phew! So now I've put that to rest, let's look at some other reasons why people are afraid to put themselves out there – all of these have been said by clients of mine over the years. While you're reading, tick the ones that you have said or used:

- Fear of what my peers might say
- Not sure what to say
- Not sure how to say what I want to say
- Not sure what platforms to be on
- Worried about looking silly
- Concerned about how my hair looks
- I'm waiting for the 'right time'
- I just haven't got the time
- I have my social media done by a VA/agency
- I need to do my make-up first
- My phone only has a back camera
- My house is messy
- Not sure if I should use my name or my business name
- Don't believe it will produce results
- It didn't work last time

- No one else is doing it that way
- I don't have a tripod
- It won't be good enough

And the list goes on.

If you've been procrastinating like this, I get it. It's usually because some kind of hidden fear is rolling around in the back of your head.

One big worry for people is about how much time it's going to take to make this happen. Let me ask you this. If you were single and you really wanted to meet someone, would you find the energy and the time to go and meet some new people? If you were married and you really wanted to make new friends, would you make the effort? If you were busy juggling your fur babies with everything else in your life but really wanted to grow your fur family, would you find a way to make it happen?

Of course you would!

If someone offered you more money than you'd ever been paid before (that might be $1,000 or $10,000 or $100,000) for a day's work, and you really needed the money, would you find the time?

Of course you would!

It does take time to do this. I'm not going to sugar coat it – you know me well enough by now to know that I'm a no B.S. kind of girl who tells it like it is. However, if you're using social media and curating a well-thought-out, strategic digital presence, it will pay off dividends for years to come.

You must make the choice, though, to get out of your own damned way! Because nobody else can do this for you if you want it done properly.

As mentioned at the start of this chapter, the other big worry for people (which compounds the worry about time) is that it has to be 'perfect'. They feel they have to make everything perfect before they put it out there, which of course takes time as they toil over it in an attempt to get it 'right'.

This could be around trying to make a downloadable document perfect before sharing, or trying to get your studio 'set' right before filming. It could be around trying to appear perfect, polished and professional.

Perfectionism is like a cancer and it ripples through everything if you don't stop it in its tracks.

Perfection is a myth

In a world that celebrates the likes of the Kardashians and the 'Real Housewives' franchises, it's understandable that so many people resist putting themselves out there because they think they're not 'there' yet or they're not good enough yet or not qualified enough.

Let's face it: these kinds of 'reality' franchises essentially propagate the stereotype of how you 'should' look when you're online. It's the same with Instagram models and 'perfect family' photos – they don't show the reality of what life is really like.

It's all a bunch of bullshit!

TRUTH BOMB #4: You don't have to show up online like you have it all together all of the time.

Your audience knows you're human. And they can smell bullshit a mile away! They're tired of having perfection rammed down their throat. Perfect families. Perfect bodies. Perfect pictures of health. Perfect homes. Perfect husbands. Perfect, perfect, perfect. They want real and they're actually demanding it. They don't want the reality TV version of 'real'. They want *real* real. They want real because they know that behind that reality TV veneer is true reality. Messy days. Good days. Up and down days.

Don't get me wrong. I'm not talking about sharing every nitty-gritty bit of your not-so-perfect life or business, or all of the unresourceful thinking that can sometimes creep in … but what I am advocating for is that you share *you*. When you've worked through a problem, share the way that you solved it, but don't do that while you're in it.

We are all a mass of imperfect perfections that not one single other person on the planet can even hope to match up to. So before we delve into how to do all of this, I'd like you to accept and acknowledge that you are not perfect and thank god for that.

I'd like you to embrace this first and foremost and then make the decision to do something different, which is to shine the light on the reality of what it's like to be in your industry, doing what you do, not just present the airbrushed version.

I also want you to understand that I get it. To this very day I still have sneaky thoughts and fears creep up and bite me on the backside:

- Who am I to do this?
- I'm such a fraud
- What if I fail?
- Will they laugh?
- What if they don't like me?
- What if I choose wrong?
- What if I do all the 'right' things and it still doesn't work?

It's normal. But what happens when you embrace imperfection and imperfect action combined with strategy is that you move through these thoughts a helluva lot quicker than if you try to run from them. You will get things done faster. You will get things done cheaper. And you will start to get results.

Let go of perfectionism and embrace all that is you. Yes, you can still make things nice and pretty. You can still have attention to detail and do the best damn job that you can, but then you need to rip off the bandaid and just get it out there!

Hiding behind perfectionism is usually masking something a bit deeper – the fear of failure. The fear of failure is insidious and it can undermine everything that you're doing before you even start.

But what if I told you that there is no failure, there is only feedback? You cannot fail. Doesn't that feel good?

The beauty with this is that you can't actually stuff this up or get it wrong, because it's all about *you* showing up in all of your glory, sharing *you*. You actually cannot fail. Isn't that liberating?

3

YOU'RE THE BOSS

OK, SO YOU NOW KNOW THAT it's got to be you who shows up, you know you need to build relationships with your audience, and you know that you are the one that your audience wants to see and get to know. What's next? How do you get started?

Great question! So glad you asked.

The first thing you need to do is change your thinking about the digital landscape and the world of social media. If you think about it as something you *have* to do (a chore and a bore) it's never going to work for you. You're not going to build a positive relationship with your audience if you are posting begrudgingly. But if you think about it as something you *want* to do, because you know it can be the key to your success and can be used as a tool to add value to your audience, you will be champing at the bit to get started.

The next thing to do is think about it as something you control, not something that controls you. It can be disillusioning when you hear intangibles such as:

- 'It's about "brand awareness"'
- 'It's about "positioning"'
- 'Something is better than nothing'
- 'The algorithms will stuff up your reach but there's nothing you can do about that'

But what if it was something that you were in control of? What if you thought about it as your very own media channel or your very own broadcasting network?

It's like the OWN (Oprah Winfrey Network) is for Oprah. She can do whatever the heck she wants over on that network because she owns it. She controls the content, the participants, the message and everything that goes on over there.

When you shift your thinking about this, you then become the owner of your own channel and you can broadcast the content that you want on it, right?

This means that you can use it as a platform for education, inspiration, motivation, for selling, for marketing yourself and other people who you support and believe in.

You'll be seen. You'll be heard. You will influence. You'll be regarded as someone who knows their stuff... and this is when you start becoming sought after.

Acting like you have a huge following is the beginning of getting a huge following.

Your own network

Now that you know why you need to start acting as if you have a huge following, it's time to get started. Release the fear of judgement. Release the fear of not being perfect. Release the fear of looking silly or stupid.

You are going to treat the entire digital world like it's your OWN network. You own every platform and you can put whatever you want out there in order for it to work for you. And there's no fear of judgement because only the people who *want* to watch and listen will tune in and the rest of the people … well, it doesn't matter what they do! They can switch channels and find someone else to listen to.

Your network is adding value out there in the market place. Remember, the way that we create value 'out there' is by putting value out there! That means solving problems that your audience has. It means showing up and getting to know your audience. Getting inside their heads and really talking to them like they're real human beings, because they are.

You'll be seen online as an expert in what you're doing. Praise the gods of the interwebs! But first, you need to own the fact that you are an expert at what you do so that you can be seen as one. Eradicating those fears as mentioned earlier is paramount to this.

You'll become sought after and this leads to you creating an impact with everything you do with your audience. They're listening. They're watching. They're resonating. They're with you all the way.

And you'll have a strategy for turning all of that into revenue or for getting that next job, or for creating the next pivot point for you. Your end game is about leveraging the work you're doing, which is about creating cashola, baby! Part 2 is all about how to make all of this happen for you.

Your inspiration mood board

All of this is well and good, however, what I know is that most people need some kind of reference point for what it is that they want to create. Much like when I have new photos taken, I need some inspiration in the form of seeing other people's photos before getting into poses! I need the reference point and the visual guides in order to then work out how to emulate what it is that I'm supposed to be doing!

Action step:

1. Research who you admire online. I'd recommend you look outside of your industry.

2. Generate a list of 10 people whom you admire.

3. Write down what it is about their profiles or presence that you like and why you like it. We tend to admire in others that which we want for ourselves. So the trick here is to tune your radar into looking for things that you like and then use that as a base point for you to use as inspiration.

4. What are the key characteristics/traits in these people?

5. Come up with a list of five words that you can use to start to embody within yourself, e.g. stylish, friendly, confident, natural, real.

One of the things that often comes up when I'm recommending this activity to people is that they tell me that they don't want to look at others in their industry for one of two reasons. Reason #1 is that they don't want to be swayed by the 'competition' and reason #2 is that they don't want to be seen as being a copycat.

I get it, which is exactly why I'd recommend that you look well outside of your industry for some inspiration. If you're an accountant, perhaps look for some interior designer influencers to follow. Maybe there are some personal trainers who inspire you. Think initially about some celebrities and how they've cultivated their online following and personal brands and how these reflect their personalities (as much as we can tell).

You could search for authors, artists, musicians or A-list stars. You might look at complementary industries, for example, if you're an interior designer, perhaps look at some of the artists you love.

The point here is that I want you to create a 'mood board' of people that you admire online so that you can use these people as a source of inspiration and motivation.

PART TWO

YOUR ZONE OF AWESOMENESS

NOW THAT WE HAVE AGREED (albeit perhaps with you kicking and screaming a little bit along the way) that you simply must get yourself out there, we need to get stuck into the nitty gritty of how we can implement this with as little pain as humanly possible as well as in the most efficient way possible. (Yes, I heard the collective sigh of relief!)

There are three parts that we're going to explore throughout this part of the book.

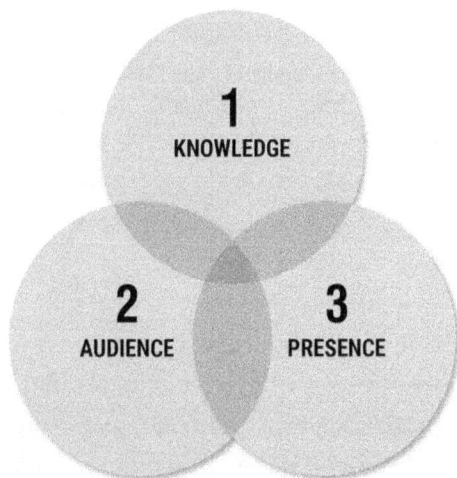

KNOWLEDGE

This is the space between your ears that houses your 'zone of awesomeness'.

Your zone of awesomeness is the thing that you do that you probably don't even realise you're doing for others. It could be the way you help people feel valued. Perhaps it's the way that you can steer a conversation back to being positive versus being negative.

We're going to explore how to use your knowledge as your super power. Because, after all, you are the best at being you.

AUDIENCE

We're going to go in depth in this part of the book to help you understand your audience. In order for you to be relevant, you've got to know who you're directing this social media stuff to otherwise it's just more noise … and dammit there's enough of that out there already.

You need to know who they are so you can start building relationships with them.

We're going to look to your audience for help so that we can solve their problems through what you're putting out there into the content-eating machine that is social media.

#relationshipsforthewin

PRESENCE

Once we have the first two segments covered, we can start the work of becoming present online. Unless you have the foundations in place before you start putting yourself out there, you can end up doing it all back to front, which equates to lost time in rework and having to retrain your audience.

The other risk you run if you jump straight to building presence is that you just end up creating more noise that blends in with the rest of the racket that's out there and nobody will know who you are.

#nothelpful

4

KNOWLEDGE

IF I SAY 'FRANKENSTEIN'S MONSTER' you get a mental image of exactly who I'm talking about, right? A man made of stitched-together body parts that somehow weirdly make him able to function.

I want you to imagine yourself like a beautiful Frankenstein's monster and that the stitched-together body pieces are all of your experiences, your knowledge, your trials, tribulations, wins, losses, success, failures and everything in between.

You are the sum of all of your parts.

Many people think that they are 'not really that special', 'boring' or that they have 'nothing of importance to share'. That's simply not true. You're far from boring and people (your ideal audience) need to hear from you and they need to be able to learn from you.

Some people even question their own value and what they bring to the table.

I call bullshit. I bet that you know more than what you think you know. In fact, I *know* you know more than you think you know.

I remember running an event with a group of clients and one of the participants wanted to walk away from the workshop with a 12-month content plan. This was no mean feat for someone who hadn't been in a room with me before! To say I was excited at the prospect was an understatement!

I took her through the process of asking her questions about her life, children, clients, beliefs and hobbies. I was using these questions to start pulling ideas out of her brain for all the different things that she could talk about, while still tying into her overall theme for the year and making sure it matched how she wanted to be seen. I started noting down all of the things she was talking about, the different topics, the things she was passionate about, the things she wanted to share with her audience – both business topics and topics that were not business-related but tied in with who she is and what she wanted to build online. We talked about the stories she would tell as part of all of that, which were based on the questions that I asked her and the answers she gave me.

From this conversation, she literally walked away with two years worth of content!
It was mapped out month by month, and week by week.

TRUTH BOMB # 5: You know more than you give yourself credit for, which is where the magic is.

At this point, people usually tell me that it's all well and good for her because she was in the room with me. Yes, she was. However, you, too, can follow the process so that you can have all of these things mapped out for you. This is exactly what you're going to do right now.

Stocktake of you

So we know the key to creating content for the digital world – including social media – is all about being you and sharing you, your stories and your experiences. There are so many things that you've done over the years and we're going to find out exactly what your zone of awesomeness is and how to use that online.

What is a stocktake (other than the ploy retailers use to get us in-store to buy all of the things we 'need' before the end of financial year)? A stocktake of you is where you go through everything in your history so that you can remind yourself about just how far you've come and, at the same time, come up with a whole lot of ideas for the content that showcases you.

As well as generating content, this stocktake is also going to help you discover and articulate your zone of awesomeness.

Gay Hendricks talks a lot about finding your 'zone of genius' in his book *The Big Leap* and he has you answer some key questions. The first one, which I love, is all about you working out what it is that you love to do the most, so much that it feels like you could do it forever without getting bored or even tired.

For me, what I love doing the most is helping people who are driven and motivated to get results using social media and digital marketing – working with people who are ready, willing and able to step up and own their space! I love the shit out of that!

We are going to work through this in the activity later, but, for now, start having a think about that for yourself. What do you love doing that doesn't feel like it takes any effort?

The other thing that is an important clue about your zone of awesomeness is identifying what people ask you for help with all the time – when they say 'You just always seem to know what to say about X' or 'You're the best at Y'.

Another clue to be on the lookout for is what you have mastered. Now, this isn't necessarily in your zone of awesomeness, however, we can use this as a foundation point when we get stuck into doing the work on social. So what have you mastered along the way?

How will this help?

I hear you asking 'But why, Nicola? Why is this important?' I'm going to tell you because you've stuck with me this far.

The key message here is that you need to learn how you can leverage every single part of you, and that includes your knowledge and all of your experiences.

Your brain is damn sexy. It's filled with information, ideas, inspiration and stories that can be shared out there with your audience to inspire, educate and motivate.

And remember, you are unique. The reason that this part is so important is that not one other person on this planet can do things in the way that you do. This is your point of difference. You are the sum of all of your experiences, your training and your modalities. It's these combined with your naturally awesome personality that will set you apart.

It's the sharing of this knowledge and expertise, combined with sharing some personal aspects of you (as much you're willing to share), that helps you to build trust and relationships. For example, a photo of you walking your dog shows others that you like to be outside, in nature and also that you're a dog person. People buy from people, so it's important that your audience feels like they can get a bit of a feeling for who you are as a person, not just as someone who wants to sell them something.

Let's get down and dirty

It's time to get down and get our hands dirty now. I know you're probably excited to get some work done, so this is what we're going to do.

Stocktake Quadrant

Time to do a stocktake of you. We're going to break this down into the following four aspects:

1. Experience (life)

2. Education and career

3. Natural gifts/talents – acknowledged

4. Innate abilities – often unacknowledged

1. Experience

To complete the stocktake for this section, I want you to take some time to back through your life and document the pivotal moments. Here are two client examples to give you an idea of how this could work for you.

Margaret is around 60 years of age. She has had the most amazing and interesting life, filled with wins, challenges and some devastating events as well as some major highs. When we started working together she was worried about how she was going to explain the transition from being a long-term corporate employee to self-employed.

I had Margaret take a look over events that had happened throughout her life – the positives and the negative ones. I asked her to consider the ones where she felt like everything was a disaster and what she did to overcome or work through those challenges, and the positive experiences that were pivotal moments, and why these were important.

Margaret, an intelligent and successful woman, was worried about the value that she was bringing to the table in her marketing online and this process helped her to see that there was value in her life experience. There was a definite point of difference between her and some of the 'spring chickens' that were out there doing similar things to her.

Thelma, on the other hand, is in her early 30s. Her worry was that she was too young and too inexperienced to be able to market herself online. I took her through a similar process and helped her to see that even though she hasn't been in business for very long, she'd been working towards this since her childhood.

She'd experienced bullying and learning difficulties as a result of undiagnosed dyslexia, along with a not-so-supportive group of people around her when she decided to change her entire life around.

I had her look at the less-than-awesome times throughout her life and what led her to the decisions and choices to make change. These things form life experience and cannot be learned or taught! You've got to experience what it's like to go through adversity.

Thelma also took a look at the positive things that had happened for her, including moving towns a few times, being brave enough to go to a new town and to a new job so that she could try her hand at something different, until she landed on her 'thing'.

Life experience doesn't just happen and it's not something you can emulate or fake.

I can promise you that even if you're in your 20s and the rest of your 'competitors' are older than you, you have value to bring to the table. Even if you're in your 60s and 'everyone else' is younger than you, you have value to bring to the table.

What pivotal moments have you had in your life that have led you to be where you are today?

I find it easier to manage this in five-year blocks. So from 20 to 25 what were your pivotal life moments? Then 25–30, 30–35, 35–40 and so on.

There's a link to download a worksheet for this and the other three stocktake aspects on my website.
www.nicolamoras.com.au/visible

2. Education and career

You may find this one a little easier as our education and most jobs
tend to stick in our minds.

I want you to go back through your education – both formal and
informal – as well as your job history and career development. Go
right back to the start and document everything you did for each role
you were in and what you learned as part of those roles.

An example of the timeline for this activity could be like mine below.

My first venture into working was at the age of about 13 when my mum
helped me start up an Avon business in my local area. I would walk from
house to house and Mum or Dad would follow me in the car while I
door knocked all of the houses asking if they wanted to order anything.

Then at the age of 16 I got my first job in a sports store that I loved.
I was also working as a manager in one of the stores that my parents
owned and did that up until about the age of 19. At my job in the
sports store I learned the practice of providing exceptional customer
service as well as the importance of having fun at work.

At 19 I started working for Westpac, one of the major banks in
Australia, and I resigned from there when I was 33. At the bank,
I learned about how much I loved helping my clients achieve their
financial goals. From investment property purchases to refinancing
their home loans to commencing investment portfolios, I found great
enjoyment in helping them save money while doing it. This is where
my love for coaching kicked in.

I started up a jewellery business when I was in my late twenties that
I was building 'on the side' to my corporate job and loved that! This
was a fun business. I learned how to buy in jewellery from overseas. I
learned how to build websites, how to use social media to promote the

business as well as how to really get out there amongst the community. I was selling jewellery locally at markets as well as wholesale around the country.

In 2010 (at the age of 32) I started my current business helping people to market themselves through building a strong personal brand. (I resigned from Westpac the following year.)

Throughout the journey of this business, I have learned so much about human behaviour, marketing, how to run a successful business along with a billion mistakes that have taken me to where I am now. I have learned the important lesson of failure and that the faster we fail, the sooner we learn and we can use those failures to improve.

Also throughout this timeline, I have gained certifications as a money coach, energy healer in different modalities, business diplomas and other qualifications.

Another example of this is a client of mine, Cait, who I have already mentioned. She is 60 years old and we've had a few conversations about the value that she brings to the table and how she can help people by showing up and marketing herself online.

She has many qualifications in psychotherapy, nursing, neuro-linguistic programming and energy work, diplomas in many modalities, and 40-plus years of experience dealing with families and individuals. When we broke that down and looked at it analytically she was able to see that she is so incredibly different to anyone else in her industry.

You may find that some of your stories and stocktake points cross over into different sections. This is OK. Please document each and every thing that you have in the timeline for each section.
Remember, also, it's not about the volume of what's in this section; it's just about getting it compiled.

3. Natural gifts/talents – acknowledged

You have so many natural gifts and talents and I trust that working through the first two steps of this stocktake process is helping you to see this!

Many people feel resistance doing this activity because it makes them take a look at *themselves* versus their experience. I want you to trust the process with this one, please.

The way you're going to do this stocktake is by looking back at your childhood to start with. I want you to document the things that you dreamed of doing and being when you were a child. Did you want to be a teacher? A dancer? On stage? Work on computers? What did you want to do and be?

When I was a child I loved performing. From the age of about three, I would put on performances for visitors to our house, except I'd call them 'customers'! I would do ballet or a dance or sing for them. As I grew older, I played schools in the cubby house with my brother and loved 'teaching' him the lesson of the day. I also remember standing on the back fence of our 2.5-acre block that overlooked acres and acres of crops and I would sing to the crops and pretend to be a television host or a famous singer or a performer. Being in front of people, and teaching or entertaining them, has always been there for me.

Leave no stone unturned for this one.

Once you've done that, I want you to move to the present and think about the types of things that your parents, your friends, your clients, your neighbours or even your children say that you're naturally great at. What do you think you're great at? *Hint: What do you get asked for help with all the time?*

4. Innate abilities – often unacknowledged

There are some things that many of us can 'just do' that we don't even realise that we can do, or we take it for granted! Some people are just naturally gifted at seeing the good in others or viewing the world as 'glass half-full' rather than half-empty.

There are two parts to this stocktake.

Part One. I want you to document what *you* think your innate gifts and talents are that are different to the things that you have been told that you are good at. For example, I think that I am pretty funny, but most people don't tell me that I'm funny!

Part Two. You're going to get BRAVE! Woohoo! You're going to take to social media to post something along the lines of this: *'Can you help me out, please? I've been set a challenge to post this and I'm a little nervous. Can you please share one word with me that you feel describes me and the impact that I have on you OR what you see as being my biggest strength? Positive words only, please! Thanks in advance.'*

I can guarantee you that you will be blown away with what others have to say about you and your strengths. There are so many people out there who admire you and I can't wait to hear the feedback from you about the feedback that you get.

When you have completed these activities, you will have a very clear picture of how awesome you are! These are the things that make you different to your competitors. These are the things that we'll draw upon when we're creating content for your platforms.

Consider the stories that relate to each of the things that you've uncovered and documented about yourself. It's unique to you and your life.

You might be surprised!

Sandy, a musician and coaching client of mine, did the activity that I've suggested that you do above. She was so surprised at the responses that she received from people and what they saw within her. There are qualities and traits that other people see in us that we sometimes just don't see in ourselves. For Sandy, this was an observation that she was driven and determined. This came as quite a shock because that wasn't how she thought about herself. Yet, upon working through the context that this person knows her in, she could see that being driven and determined is absolutely her, it just took some thinking to see it from a different perspective.

There is no one out there who has lived the exact same trajectory as you. I'm proud of you for working through that activity.

You can see by this evidence that there are going to be very few people on the planet who are going to be able to communicate in the way that you do, right?

Now you've done the stocktake, you can see why a social media manager or a virtual assistance or even an agency can't do this for you. They're not you and it's impossible for someone else to mimic your voice and echo your experiences.

We are going to use all of these points you've come up with on the worksheets to generate ideas for content and stories that will demonstrate your expertise and point of difference in the market place.

Working out what to share

Most people I work with struggle to come up with what to share and how much to share online.

I want to step you through an activity I get every client of mine to complete. It's called the Disco Ball Activity.

THE DISCOBALL!!

A disco ball has many mirrors on it, right? There are countless facets and each one shines back a little differently.

Much like a human. Multifaceted. The interesting thing that I've found over the years is that each person you come into contact with is going to be drawn to you for a different reason and it's impossible to predict what facet of you someone is going to be drawn in by.

Different people will resonate with different things within you. Some people resonate with me because I'm a mother of three and I'm a business owner. Some people love that I love Louis Vuitton and camping and find the idea of me in a tent with my trackies on, peeing behind a bush in the middle of nowhere hilarious! Others resonate with me because of the results I get. Others like my 'realness' because I pull no punches!

What happens after they're drawn in is they start to learn more about what I actually do and the problems that I solve for people. But they all want to know *me* at some level first and foremost.

For you, it could be the fact that you love talking about self-care in corporate. It could be that you love to ride your bike everywhere if you can, even to high-powered meetings. It could be that you're an introvert and you detest networking events but you do them anyway!

The next activity is going to give you limitless ideas for content for social media.

Imagine that the above image is a disco ball and that this disco ball represents you in all your glory and with all of your contrasts. You're going to fill each of those mirrors in with different things that you like.

For example, if it were my disco ball, I'd put 'five-star accommodation' on the left hand side in one of the tiles. I love love *love* luxury hotels. I also love camping (OK, it's more glamping, but you get the idea) and I would fill that in one of the tiles on the opposite side of the disco ball. I love designer stores, so I might put Louis Vuitton in one facet on the right-hand side, and then K-Mart on the left-hand side, cause I love the heck out of that store, too!

I'd like you to think about the following categories when you're filling this in:

- Fun

- Social

- Family

- Business/career

- Soul/beliefs/religion

- Finances

- Health

- Mindset

- Relationships

What do you love doing or talking about in each of these categories? What are you passionate about?

See! You're amazing and multifaceted and super interesting. We're going to use some of this in the next part of the book so keep it handy.

Content ideas aplenty

What you're starting to see by now is that there are many things that make you different and you actually have loads of things that you can write about, talk about and share online in a way that is unique to you, your experiences and your zone of awesomeness.

When we look at people online we make a pretty quick decision when it comes to deciding if we're going to listen to them or not. If we're completely honest, it probably happens within seconds of landing on a person's profile or website. This is what people are going to do with you, too, which is why you want to really determine the things that make you different – based on you and your qualities, your way of life, the philosophy that you live by and even your likes and dislikes.

Here are just two examples of how this worked for me.

In 2015 I had some posts and advertising on Facebook about my *Rich Bitch Guide to Having it All* and it got a lot of interaction. A lady by the name of Kelly-Ann came across this ad and requested a copy of the guide. She also requested to have a conversation with a team member of mine about becoming a client. In between us calling her and speaking with her, she went through every photo on my Facebook page. She liked what she saw!

The following day she enrolled to join the mastermind program I was running at the time and I had a conversation with her. I asked her what was it about me that resonated with her. She told me that it was the photos of travel and the photos of me at Louis Vuitton, and the lifestyle posts that I put up – like walking with my children in the mornings. She told me loved the overall feeling that was created when she looked through my posts.

By comparison, another client of mine, Michelle, told me that she was drawn to me because of my lifestyle – the photos of me camping and being out in nature, spending quality time with the people I loved – as well as the 'business stuff'.

People will be drawn to you for so many different reasons and we can't always predict what that reason will be, so it's important to identify each of these aspects of us.

It's almost like being able to look in a super clean mirror that reflects exactly who you are – your genius, your quirks, your natural talents and your learned ones – when you've been looking through a dirty one for such a long time.

Time to own your awesomeness and celebrate these new eyes.

But how does this help you?

All of these things that you've shared in your disco ball and within each section of the stocktake quadrant are ideas that you can use for content. Yes. Content!

Remember, people are humans first and humans buy from humans that they like!

In the next chapter we're going to talk about how to make this relevant to your audience and how we can use these stocktake items as pivot points to solve problems that your audience have.

What this means is that you'll have the inspiration for creating content easily (because it comes from within you). It means that you'll be able to solve problems for people, so you're adding value, and we know that this then leads to your audience trusting you which then leads to them buying from you or hiring you.

ACTIVITIES TO COMPLETE IF YOU HAVEN'T ALREADY:

1. Write down what you LOVE doing

2. Write down what everyone asks you for help with

3. Stocktake each section of the Stocktake Quadrant

4. Post on Facebook or email your friends and ask them what they think your strengths are (do not give them any hints)

5. Disco Ball activity

6. List some things that you love talking about/could talk about that may fall into the outlined nine categories

You can download activity sheets at www.nicolamoras.com.au/visible

5

AUDIENCE

I WANT YOU TO IMAGINE FOR A MOMENT that you go to a bar with the intention of finding someone to talk to, but rather than scoping it all out, you walk in and start shouting at the top of your voice that you want to find someone to connect with. You can imagine the looks that you'd get from most of the people in there, right? They'd be thinking you were more than just a little 'special' or crazy!

You've probably seen bakeries in shopping malls doing this exact thing. Their younger staff standing in a crowded shopping mall with their little breadbasket filled with bite-size samples that they're handing out to all and sundry.

Here's the thing. NOBODY WANTS THE DAMN BREAD!

The people who are having these things shoved down their throats may not even be hungry! Or like bread! Or have any intention of buying anything at all. Just because the bakery is giving away free samples to every person they possibly can, it doesn't mean that these people are automatically going to hand over their cold hard cash or whip out their credit cards and get all tap-happy. It doesn't mean that they're going to become a customer. Or a client. Or that they're ever going to set foot in your store or visit your website.

What so many businesses don't realise is that it's not about the size of the audience (or increasing the volume of the foot traffic) that matters on its own. It's what you do with it that counts.

It's not just a numbers game whereby we try to convince as many people as possible to buy our stuff or accept our free samples. It's about specifically targeting the right audience, with the right offer, with the right solution for them.

A scattergun approach doesn't work. Not everyone wants your bread even if they are hungry!

This chapter is all about finding your ideal audience and creating a communication strategy that works for them, that has you communicating with strength and with intention.

This is where you can become more efficient and actually more powerful with your social media than ever before, because you're not going for the 'let's be seen every-damn-where' approach. You're going to be super specific in order to capture (and retain) the attention of your ideal audience – your niche.

Let's be seen by the people who count. Let's get stuck into it.

Communication

Communication is a two-way street but for some reason people often forget this when they are marketing themselves online. They think that having a conversation with their audience can be automated – or even worse: one-sided. It's not how it works.

Automation on social media is boring and disrespectful to your audience. There are some things that we can automate and others that we simply cannot.

One of the things that infuriates me right now is the use of bots to send automatic messages to connections or followers. On Twitter it's the 'thumbs up' that you get from people who start following you, or the direct message to your inbox that is the furthest thing from personalised as you can get. On Instagram, it's the automated 'thumbs up' or comments like 'I've checked your profile and I love it. Let's connect'. These are automatic posts. They're rude. They're disrespectful and full of bullshit. They're not real people interacting with you, these profiles have a program set up that 'likes' posts with particular keywords or phrases or hashtags. It's why sometimes you see your followers grow one day and then the next day they're gone! They unfollowed you because a social media bot was set up to like your page for just one day based on the words that you used in the post.

If you want to feel heard, then you can rest assured that your audience also wants this. If you want to feel valued, then you need to not only value but also respect your audience. You cannot automate that.

The only way that you can do this is if you know your audience better than they know themselves. This is important because it means you can step into their shoes and work out what they're thinking and feeling. Then you can create content for them that is helpful and connective. One of the overwhelmingly obvious things that is missing in the world of social media and online these days is empathy for one's audience. And we need to change that.

Some facts:

- You need to know your audience first and foremost, otherwise all you're doing with your posts and blogs and videos is actually contributing to the social media noise pollution index (totally made up by me, but you get the point).

- You can spend all the time you like stocktaking your knowledge, working out what stories you can tell in order to demonstrate a clear and concise point of view, but if you don't know who you're talking to, then it will be a totally pointless activity. And I know that you don't have any more time to waste doing things that aren't helpful.

- While knowing your audience intimately is really important, it's also imperative that you don't assume that you know them! I know. I've done it and it always bites me on the backside!

So it's critical that you communicate with your audience in a way that's going to resonate with them. In order to do that, you need to know who they are.

Who's your niche?

The first thing you need to decide on is who your audience is. 'An inch wide and a mile deep' is the best way to describe an ideal niche.

STEP 1 – Identify your niche

I want you to think of an ideal client (or an ideal boss if you're in a job). Base them on the best client you've ever worked with – someone that you could clone. This person is going to be your niche audience.

- Give them a name
- Give them a gender and age
- What do they do for a living?
- What is their relationship status?
- If they have a partner, what does the partner do for a living?
- Do they have children?
- Where do they live?
- What kind of car do they drive?
- What are their goals and dreams?
- What are their stress points?
- What do they really not like about their life?
- What is their health like?
- What is their mindset like?
- What is their financial situation? (Hint: I'd make it so that they're not broke unless you're operating a charity. You need people to be able to pay you!)
- What's the 3 am story that they tell themselves about the worst-case scenario? (And how this relates to what you do.)

For example, my 'ideal client' in 2015 was a 37-year-old entrepreneur by the name of Olivia

Name: Olivia

Age and gender: 37-year-old woman

What they do for a living: entrepreneur

Relationship status: married

Partner's job: husband is employed FT and earns $150k+ per year. Is sometimes away but not often enough for it to be a problem.

Children: two

Where they live: in the burbs

Car they drive: a Jeep. Husband has a company car as well.

Goals and dreams:
She's been building her business and initially it started out as a way to bring in a little bit of extra money, but she's since been bitten by the bug. The entrepreneur bug!

She's been getting 1:1 clients and that's going well. She knows she wants to grow, but she doesn't know what she wants that to look like.

She wants to lift her business to $1m per year. She's happy to lift to $500k at this point.

She dreams of having an international client base that travel to her (and occasionally she'll travel overseas) so she can spend more time with her family.

She intrinsically knows that this isn't going to be the thing that makes her happy, but she knows it will certainly create a lot more opportunities for her to do more of what she wants.

She's chatted to a few of her friends and they've all told her that she's nuts! She should 'just be happy with what she has', but she's not. So, instead of talking with them even more about what she wants to create, she keeps it inside.

Mindset:
She's a go-getter. Driven. Ambitious ... but she's also a little bored. She's a creative. She's a visionary as well as a hustler! She'll do what it takes when she knows what she wants.

Stress points:
She has no more hours to sell. Wants more clients to help but there's no room. She's frustrated and tired.

Her husband tells her to do whatever it is that she needs to do to change the situation because he wants his happy wife back. The kids are hanging for more attention, but she's so time-poor and feels guilty for not spending the time with them that they want ... yet ... she can't take the foot off, otherwise everything implodes.

She's done 'everything' and tried 'everything' and searched for 'everyone' ... she's been looking for a better way. She knows there must a better way but can't even imagine the next steps.

She's intuitive with other people and with what they need to hear so why can't she use her intuition for herself? She's great at doing this for everybody else, but can't seem to tap into the 'thing' that's going to make it work and take it up a level.

Truthfully, she wants to reinvent herself. She wants to lead with strength. She wants to find the people who really need her and do the things that she does best.

What they really don't like about their life:
Honestly. She's a bit pissed off with it all. She is getting busier and busier and daren't take the foot off the pedal because she doesn't want the momentum to decrease.

She's stuck on the carousel of sameness and doesn't know how to break out.

She doesn't love how her business is working anymore. She was in love with it initially and now … it's feeling like a lot of work.

She can't articulate what she wants.

She can't articulate what she wants to create.

She can't describe what it is … but she knows there's something missing.

Health:
She's not really happy with her health overall.

She feels like she's always running out of time and doesn't really get the time to focus on her physical activity.

Doesn't exercise anywhere near as much as she should and wants to.

She doesn't take time out for self-care.

Eats pretty healthily but still has days where she can't be bothered and just eats whatever she can get her hands on.

Financial situation:
Her business is going well but she wants more.

Her husband has a well-paid job so they don't need to worry about money.

She needs to be making money, though, to contribute to the financial household.

She wants more.

She has goals of creating half-a-million dollars per year to a million dollars per year in revenue and then growing from there.

She does have money blocks though and feels like she's going around and around the money merry-go-round and wants to get off it.

The 3 am story that they tell themselves about the worst-case scenario and how this relates to what I do:

Worrying about her business and if it's going to be able to reach the heights that she dreams about.

She worries about the time she's sacrificing with her children to grow the business and hopes that it's going to pay off.

She worries about her husband growing along with her in terms of mindset and what happens if he doesn't.

She's worried about making more money in her business because her husband has been talking about joining her to work in her business.

What if it all comes crashing down?

What if she loses it all?

STEP 2 – Interview people who fit your niche

We discussed earlier the importance of not making assumptions and we need to spend some time speaking with people who fit your ideal niche.

I recommend putting a post up on your social media profiles asking something along the lines of this:

> *HELP! Can you help me out? I've been spending some time working on my business recently and I've been set a challenge to interview 10 people who fit the following points:*
>
> ... insert a few key points that describe your niche audience.

Here are some examples:

Example one (a niche audience for a business consultant):

• Business owner

• 35–40 years of age

• Been in business for 2+ years

• Struggling with social media in some way

• Motivated individual

Example two (a niche audience for a personal trainer):

• Feeling overweight

• 28–33 years of age

• Wants to lose 5–10 kg

• Struggled in the past with yo-yo dieting

• Tired of the latest fad diet, just wants something that works

Example three (a niche audience for a graphic designer):

- Business owner

- 42–50 years of age

- Started up any kind of business in the last year

- Struggles with graphic design – has played with Canva

- Unhappy with current branding

- Needs a website design that fits them, wants a logo and new business cards

Then finish off with:

If that sounds like you, please send me a message because I'd love to interview you for some market research I'm doing. Don't worry, I'm not selling a thing, I just want to make sure I'm on the right track.

Thanks in advance

You'll be amazed at the volume of people who respond. Humans love helping other humans and this gives them the perfect opportunity to do this for you.

Here are the interview questions for the ten people who fit your audience parameters.

1. Tell me a bit about yourself and what you do.

2. What are your goals?

3. What are your biggest challenges when it comes to [insert your topic/business/what you do in here]?

4. Where do you see yourself in the next 12 months?

5. What motivates you to keep going?

6. Do you feel like there's anything else you'd like to share with me based on what we've discussed today?

Conclude the interview with a very sincere and heartfelt thank you. Do not sell them anything. Don't talk to them about your program or your offer or your products! Keep this interview super clean and just be grateful that they've shared themselves with you.

Once you have done that, collate the answers and you'll start to see some commonalities between your people, which you can start using for content ideas online.

STEP 3 – 54 Problem Activity

This is where you're going to whip out a notepad or a notebook and list all of the problems that your person has. I call this the 54 Problem Activity.

I literally do this every time I work with a client and every time I decide to 're-niche'. I sit and list every single problem that they have. People have problems, stressors and things that they worry about and these are the things that you need to clearly identify before you go out to market.

For example, if you're a book editor and your niche is a first-time business book author, the thinking/stressors/problems that this person has are probably going to be something along the lines of:

1. I don't know how to edit my own work.

2. How do I know if what I'm sharing is too much or not?

3. How do I choose an editor?

4. What's the timeline?

5. What if my writing is shit?

6. What if it sounds stupid?

7. What if the person who edits book doesn't 'get' me or understand my message?

8. What does an editor actually DO?

9. I'm busy juggling my work and my kids – how much will I need to rework?

10. I'm really not getting enough sleep – how I am going to find the time and space to do this properly?

11. I'm a cup-half-full kind of person, but I'm really scared that this isn't going to be any good.

12. How many rounds of editing are there?

13. Will they introduce me to a publisher?

14. My partner doesn't like what I've written.

15. When do I engage them?

16. Should I send my manuscript to my friends first?

17. Do I present it to them in Word?

18. What if my computer crashes while I'm writing?

19. I hope my clients like it, but what if they don't?

20. This is going to be used for positioning; what if it doesn't work?

21. I want to write something I can be proud of.

22. I want to write something my children will be proud of.

23. What if I can't sell any books?

24. What if people laugh at it and think it's juvenile?

Another example might be for a yoga instructor whose niche is over-50s beginners. The thinking/stressors/problems of this person might be:

1. What will the class be like?

2. What do I wear?

3. What if I can't move into the positions?

4. Will they teach me or am I supposed to know the basics?

5. Do I eat beforehand?

6. Do I have to take my own mat?

7. Will we meditate? I hate meditating!

8. What if I pass wind?

9. Do I take a friend?

10. How many people will be there?

11. I'm so busy: how do I know I'll like it rather than just wasting my time?

12. Will I be able to keep up?

13. Will the moves be in English?

14. Do I seriously have to downward dog?

15. I can't tell my kids about this, they'd laugh at me!

Here are the problems and stressors that I imagined for my ideal client – 'Olivia':

1. Wants to transition her business

2. Wants to evolve but doesn't know how to position it

3. Fear of success

4. Fear of failure

5. Worried that nothing will change

6. Worried that everything will change

7. Marketing is an issue

8. Doesn't know what she doesn't know

9. Wants to write a book but doesn't know how

10. Wants balance

11. Wants success

12. Doesn't know what the next step is

13. Doesn't have a plan

14. Feels like she's going to crash and burn: it's just a matter of when

15. Wants to re-niche to a 'better' niche

16. Can't take on any more 1:1

17. Doing everything right now

18. Diary is full = income capped

19. Cannot work any extra hours

20. Has forgotten what her MAGIC is

… the list went on, but you get the idea.

At this point, it's not about the problems that you will solve for them, it's more about getting a very robust picture about this person and what their whole life is looking like, right now, before they work with you.

STEP 4 – Disco Ball Activity for your niche

Remember the Disco Ball Activity you did for yourself? Awesome! You're also going to do this for your ideal audience, please.

Fill in the facets for them based on what you already know about your audience from the interview you've already done, and what you've learned about your audience.

If your ideal niche was the over-50s beginner yoga student for example, their disco ball mirrors may be filled in like this:

- Likes to hang out with friends
- Likes to spend time alone
- Loves going on off-road drives in nature
- Loves being in the city
- Likes Lululemon clothing
- Loves the Cotton On tee
- Enjoys tea
- Loves champagne
- Hates the phone
- Loves the phone

If your ideal niche was the person writing the business book:

- Loves work
- Loves down-time
- Enjoys being busy
- Likes solitude
- Loves being around people

- Appreciates own company
- Loves Target
- Loves luxury goods
- Loves fine dining
- Loves fast food
- Enjoys being in active wear
- Loves dressing up

So now you have a pretty solid idea of your niche. You know their problems, you know what they are looking for, and you know you are able to help them.

Here's what happens when you start embracing the idea of speaking to one specific person with your posts:

- You're consistent with your message
- You're solving problems so you're seen as an expert in what you're doing
- You're not actually telling people that you're brilliant and amazing and insightful and helpful, but they can see that from everything that you're putting out there
- You inspire confidence
- People engage with you
- People start asking more questions, which will lead to them asking buying questions (yay!)

Are you ready to get started?

Let's make it happen

There are four things you need to do to make this happen.

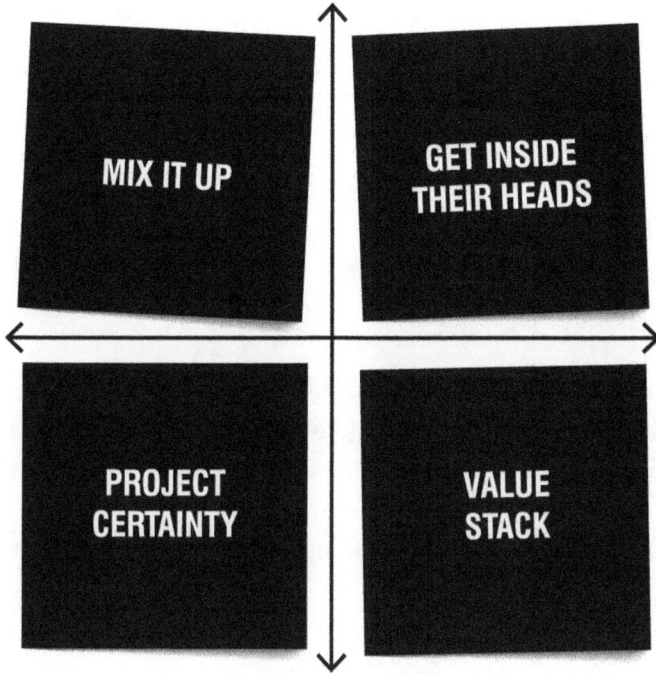

1.MIX IT UP – Communication strategy

2.GET INSIDE THEIR HEADS – Rapport

3.PROJECT CERTAINTY – Stance

4.VALUE STACK – Influence

Let's look at each one individually.

1. MIX IT UP – Communication strategy

Having a communication strategy that builds relationships online is critical to being visible online. The key to a successful communication strategy is to mix up your methods, because people take in information in different ways.

Some people are highly visual so they'll need to see pictures of you, and of the kinds of things you do with and for people, so they can see what it is that you're all about.

Others process information more effectively by listening. You'll reach them by putting out audios and/or videos. These could range from podcasts to audio snippets, videos to Facebook Live broadcasts to webinars.

Other people prefer something more tangible. So it is great if you have things that they can print out or download and work on. Books, checklists and that kind of thing is super helpful for these people.

To make sure you're communicating effectively, you need to embrace all of these communication methods with the content that you're putting out online.

2. GET INSIDE THEIR HEADS – Rapport

This is where all your work on your niche comes in. Now you know your ideal client's goals and dreams, their problems and challenges, you can put yourself into their shoes and determine the kinds of things that they're thinking, feeling and worrying about.

The more you talk about these and offer solutions, (you will share with them what they *need to do* solve it, not necessarily *how* they will do it – more on that later) the more they're going to view you as an expert and, more importantly, as someone that they can trust.

3. PROJECT CERTAINTY – Stance

This is all about you, baby! Your inner confidence shining through. You're out there in all of your glory.

I am not a fan of 'faking it till you make it'. In fact, I think it's total bullshit. You don't have to fake anything. Let's face it. The stocktakes you did in the last chapter are evidence that you are awesome (not that you need the evidence to prove it, but it helps, right?)

The way to embody this stance of certainty is to remind yourself of who you are.
Remind yourself that you have immense value to offer, that you have the knowledge, experience and know-how to make a damn huge impact.

Use that as reinforcement for that stance of certainty online while you are out there solving problems for this audience of yours.

4. VALUE STACK – Influence

I touched on value stacking in Chapter One: now it's time to get into it. I coined the term 'value stacking' around 2012 when I was writing the curriculum for a course about how to use social media to build audience and generate leads.

Value stacking is my online relationship-building version of the trust account metaphor that Stephen R Covey talks about in his book *7 Habits Of Highly Effective People*. Value stacking is where you keep adding more and more value into the marketplace in the form of free content that is easily accessible. Some content will require people to opt-in in order to access the information, for example by providing their name and email address in exchange for receiving the free piece of content, and other content will be free for all and sundry to find and consume with little commitment other than their attention.

The way value stacking works for me is that I don't want to always be selling to my audience because I think that's pretty disrespectful. I want to build relationships and rapport and sell to them occasionally and when it makes sense to.

So how do you value stack?

In part one I talked about working through the relationship-building timeline using 'know you, like you, trust you' strategies. Pattie was doing this for her boss earlier on in this book.

Imagine that you have your Facebook page in front of you (or any other platform for that matter). I'd like you to imagine that you have five posts up on that page.

For example:

1. A post that is just text
2. A picture of you out and about getting through your day
3. A post that is a video – either of you or another video you've found somewhere in the world of online
4. A post that is a quote picture/or a meme-type post
5. And then perhaps another text post

Now imagine that you put up a post where you're offering something – something for people to buy, download or participate in like a webinar. Something that requires them to opt-in. I call this a 'call-to-action' post.

If you're value stacking throughout everything that you do, imagine you get one point for each post you put up. This means you can put one call-to-action post up without feeling like you're always selling something (even if it's just offering a free give away or download or training).

Some people will lap all of that up and then make the decision to invest. Others will keep stalking you, I mean *following* you, like what happened with Cait earlier.

Makes sense, huh?

You're on your way

Now, all of that is awesome, right? But wait, there's more! There are two more brilliant things that happen when you post this way.

First, you start to build your position as someone who knows their stuff and as someone people want to get to know more. This is how you start to get attention. And you haven't even been shouting at anyone; you're just solving problems!

And of course getting attention means increasing your visibility.

KABLAM! This is what you were hoping for, right? And we haven't got into how you build presence yet!
Second, you start to build your ideal audience. It's not about the size of the audience; it's about creating a real connection and rapport with the people who form that audience.

And that is worth its weight in gold.

ACTIVITIES TO COMPLETE IN THIS CHAPTER:

1. Find your niche by creating your ideal client – a fictitious person that you name and describe in detail

2. Interview ten people who fit your audience parameters

3. 54 Problem Activity for your niche audience

4. Disco Ball Activity for your niche audience

You can download activity sheets at www.nicolamoras.com.au/visible

6

PRESENCE

LET ME TELL YOU ABOUT JEROMY.

He had tried six or seven business ideas and ventures while working as a school teacher in regional New South Wales before landing on this one: *Rewiring Children's Brains for Better Learning*.

The problem was that he didn't know how to market himself and his business. He had tried more traditional methods such as newspaper advertising and cold calling. He'd tried approaching other schools but to no avail.

He saw an advert on Facebook for a 'Facebook for Business' workshop that I was running in 2014 and decided to come along with his wife, Kim. Jeromy is the kind of guy who is willing to try anything if he's seen that it's worked for others before him.

He was nervous about putting his face out there, because he didn't really have an audience yet nor the confidence to really create a splash online. So he took it slowly, working through everything step by step. Now, he has more than 12,000 people who receive his emails. He has more than 14,000 people who follow him on his page.

He is visible. He is growing in confidence every week and doing more of the things that showcase his personality, his quirks and his humour.

Was he scared of doing it? Yes.

Was he worried about what others would think? Sometimes.

Did he let that hold him back? HELL NO!

I think the thousands of people he helps every single day thank goodness for the fact that he just got there and started building his presence.

Now it's your turn.

Where to begin

You need to meet your audience where they are at.

OK, so you now know who your audience is, and you know what to do to get their attention to build a relationship with them, but how on earth do you know where to do this? There are about a bazillion platforms to choose from, each with their very own set of quirks and twists and benefits and of course, downsides.

Let's take a quick stocktake of the major platforms you can use to get yourself out there:

- Facebook
- LinkedIn
- Twitter
- Instagram
- Blogging on your website
- Vlogging on your website
- Guest blogging
- Podcasting
- YouTube
- Snapchat

There are so many different places and ways that you can get yourself out there; how do you know which to choose?

There's a myth that you need to be across all platforms in order to be visible. It's not true. You do not need to use all of them (is that a sigh of relief I hear?)

You do, however, need to use some of them strategically and in a way that is going to help you to connect with your audience. And you know who they are right? So that's going to help you choose.

I'm going to get you to start with a baseline of three and then work up from there if needed. And to make it even easier for you, I've chosen the first two platforms: Facebook and either blogging or vlogging on your website, so you only have to chose one! Yay! Aren't you lucky?

The reason I'm choosing Facebook for you (and it's got to be a business page otherwise you run the risk of Facebook shutting you down, which means you've just lost all of that amazing stuff you've been putting up), is because 2.2 billion people are on there every month. They're spending 40 minutes per day on average on the platform killing time! (I know, it's sacrilege!) But you, my friend, can be the source of that distraction and time killing. #winning!

In addition, people want to feel like they can connect with you on a more personal level, and Facebook is the premier platform for that.

An important thing to note is that many people will not click 'like' or comment because they don't want their friends seeing what they're interacting with. Some will, but just be aware that many won't. It doesn't mean they're not watching.

The second platform is your website because it gives people a place (without being distracted by other people!) to research you and get to know you. It gives them another way outside of social media to hear what you have to say about your area of expertise.

Your website helps to share a lot more facets of you than social media does, as well. You can have a page for testimonials, a page for how people can work with you, a blog page (I hope this comes as no surprise to you!) and can offer different ways of learning from you via giving away free information. Secondary to this, it's also another way for people to get in touch with you.

I make the third platform your choice because you know who your people are and the platform that they're most likely to be on outside of Facebook.

For example:

- A business accountant is less likely to post photos on Instagram to try to appeal to their audience, they'd use LinkedIn to leverage a professional relationship
- An artist or designer probably isn't going to use LinkedIn because people want to see images of the work that they're doing. Instagram is a perfect platform for them

Moral of the story, here, is that you need to know who your audience is (lucky we did that work in the previous chapter!) and where they're hanging out.

What to post, where and why

FACEBOOK

Facebook is great for any kind of posts. From short text to long, with or without images. The medium that Facebook is looking for more of is video (see below for more on this). The more you can give Facebook what it wants, the better off you're going to be.

Facebook is very much a 'let's kill some time' platform. So you want to put content up there that is going to create a pattern interrupt for people – something that is going to make people stop and look.

For example, if you're a home-renovating consultant, you could use various Facebook posts to show before-and-after progress shots. You can share the behind-the-scenes action. Photos of you out shopping for the window dressings and the home decor. You can share the process with choosing tiles and why you chose what you chose.

Remember, your people are on Facebook. And, honestly, if you do the numbers, if your average sale per client is $1,000 per year, you only need 100 people out of the entire world to buy from you and you'll make $100k. That's 100 people out of the 2.2 billion who are on the platform.

Not bad numbers, really!

FACEBOOK LIVE

I've listed this as a separate point because it's a really important feature that you can use for free. It can really extend your reach.

Facebook is pushing its live video function because it wants to take over the YouTubes when it comes to video. And the more you can give the beast that is Facebook what it wants, the better it is for you. You end up being rewarded generally with increased reach on your other posts, which means that more of your Facebook audience gets advised that you have new content up.

Facebook Live is a tool within the Facebook app that means you can 'go live' at any given time and your fans or likers will be notified. In the Facebook app on your phone, when you want to create a new post, you'll see the option to 'Go Live'. When you press this, you will see a preview and then you can press 'Go Live' and you'll be on the air. There are no limitations with time that you can be live for, using the Facebook app.

An example for a restaurant owner could be an 'in-action' video of the kitchen preparing the food for the night ahead. They could share some 'secret' hints and tips to preparing food like a professional that would inspire future diners and perhaps budding chefs.

INSTAGRAM

Instagram is the place for images and short videos. It's very geared towards products and memes. It's a wonderful place for you to be present if your ideal audience is under 30. The tide is slowly turning and more of the older age brackets are starting to play in there, however, its primary audience is the under-30s.

You would be well placed to put a link to something free that people can opt-in and download within the bio section of your profile on Instagram. Then, when you're posting in Instagram, you can say something along the lines of 'click link in bio' and that will direct your audience to a landing page where they can give you their information.

If you're a graphic designer and you believe your audience is on Instagram, then you could post photos of things that inspire you. Share your lifestyle. Share your mood boards. Share your client work.

Your call to action could be to download something interesting and relevant that you've created such as the 'Ultimate guide to creating the perfect logo'. In order to receive this free guide, they need to provide their email address and they go into your email database (more on this later).

INSTAGRAM TV (IGTV)

This is a recent addition to the Instagram suite of services. You can create a video and upload it so that people can view it within the IGTV app or through Instagram. There is a ten-minute time limit at the moment on videos you can share on IGTV.

If you're a cake decorator you could do a video on how you decorate cakes in your style. You could talk about the projects you're working on and how to hire you.

LINKEDIN

LinkedIn certainly has some lower numbers in terms of daily active users; however, it's still a great platform on which to create a presence. Shorter posts, videos with captions and links to blogs and articles are brilliant for LinkedIn.

Keep in mind that people are only on there for on average 10 minutes per day, so be smart and strategic about the length and type of content you share on here.

If you're an author, you could use LinkedIn posts to talk about your book and the problems that it solves or addresses. You can share the process that you went through in writing your book. Post about why it's important for your audience to purchase it and read it.

VLOGGING

Vlogging means video blogging, which is where you record a content-rich video and you upload it to your website. A vlog can be any length of time you like. You just have to make sure you get the message across!

I recommend following a structure for your vlogs:
- Briefly introduce what you're going to talk about

- Introduce yourself

- Share the reason why they need to learn this lesson or why this is important. For example: 'Everyone we talk to at the moment is having trouble baking cookies without wheat flour'.

- Talk about the issue or the situation in depth by sharing a story with them either about you or about a client you've worked with

- Give them the solution or the steps that they need to work through in order to help them

Tell them what they need to do now = call to action

YOUTUBE

YouTube is the video content hub of the world until Facebook takes it over! YouTube is great for housing your video blogs before you embed them into your website.

YouTube is used by more and more people for research and entertainment.

I would recommend you have a YouTube channel and start getting some videos up on there.

PODCASTING

Podcasts are great if your audience are commuters, business owners, career people and people who love to multitask because they can have the audio playing in the car or in their ears while they're doing something else.

Podcasts can go for as long as they need to go for in order for you to get your message across!

Let's say that you're a business consultant and you help businesses get from $20m to $50m in revenue. You can talk about the challenges that CEOs face when they look after that level of organisation. You might be passionate about leadership and self-care. You can share stories about your clients (being discreet, of course).

TWITTER

Twitter is a great platform for celebrities and journalists, but maybe not so great for crafty entrepreneurs and business people such as you. In my history of doing this work I have only heard of one lady who uses it effectively to create conversations. She is a guest writer for a lot of newspapers though!

SNAPCHAT

Snapchat is an interesting platform. I have not personally used it for business but have heard of people who have. Again, where your audience is spending time will dictate the choice of platform to use.

Remember, with all of the platforms, solve your audience's problems and you'll be good to go.

Consistency

'Why do we need to be across at least three platforms?' is the question I'm usually asked at this point in time.

There's a simple answer, and a more nuanced answer.

The simple answer is that when people are actively looking for someone to help them this gives them multiple places to find you.

The nuanced answer is that people are going to research you. They'll probably go over to the Googles and 'search you up' as my kids would say. They'll go to Facebook and look up your name. They'll look at your business page. They'll do the same in LinkedIn. The same in Instagram. They'll look at your website. They'll internet-stalk you. Not in a weird way. Just to get the full picture. (The number of people who have asked me over the years at different times if I'm OK because I forgot to post a morning walk photo is hilarious and not at all creepy!)

So you need to be there when they go looking. And more than that, you need to be consistent.

What I know from everything that I've done over the years, and from seeing what my successful clients do, and what some of my peers have done, is that consistently showing up is the key to building trust and rapport with an audience.

I have not a doubt in my body that, like me, my clients and peers have bad days and good days and so-so days. Yet, every day they still show up. Every day I show up. Because it's not about painting the perfect picture of the perfect life, it's about being real and sharing the message even when it's hard. Even when it's uncomfortable. Because at the end of the day, it's about helping your audience reach the heights that they want – it's not really about you.

Now let's add another layer of visibility to this consistency.

You may have heard of sales funnels or marketing funnels. This is the tool we use to bring people together into one place so we can build a relationship with them.

I call this the 'funnel of trust'.

Imagine that all the ways you connect with people on your three or more platforms overarches the top section of the funnel. What you want to do is find a way to get them inside your funnel. Inside that top section there. You can do this by collecting a name and an email address in exchange for a piece of valuable content or training (remember value stacking?) Using this process, you can be seen in their inboxes as well as in their social media feeds.

From there you keep adding value, getting them further into your funnel of trust.

In Chapter One I mentioned that 75% of people require seven to ten touch points from you prior to making a decision to opt-in or buy from you. This is because they are trying to discern if you are one of the 'sharks', if it's spin or if you are actually able to do what you say. The further they go into your funnel of trust, the more sure they will be that you are genuine and can actually help them. As you keep adding value you will build enough trust and desire for your solution that they will eventually purchase something from you.

This happens in the bottom section.

Along the way, some people will stop listening to you, which is fine!

Some people will learn and listen more from you, which is great!

What you could offer

Free things you could give away in exchange for the name
and email address include:

- A 3-step guide
- A 4-part video training series
- A free checklist
- An ebook
- A webinar training session.

Some examples of things that I or my clients have given away
that have achieved great results:

- *How to Rewire your Child's Brain for Improved Learning* –
  delivered as a live webinar training
- *The Rich Bitch Guide to Having it All* – a three-part PDF
  guide
- *The Smart Girl's Guide to Reinventing her Career* – a PDF
  guide
- *Leadership Hacks* – four-part email series – a PDF guide
- Social Media Strategy Guide – a planner that was sent out
  along with a three-part training series
- *Business Toolbox* – a PDF guide
- *Three Steps to Choosing your Next Graphic Designer* – a
  PDF guide
- *Ten Steps to Stronger Legs* – a PDF guide
- *Use your Energetic Field to Grow your Finances* – a live
  webinar training

Content is king

I'm so pleased you've made it this far and you're realising that you have so much power right at your fingertips to build the kind of visibility that you want to create for your own personal brand, your business or yourself.

To recap swiftly:

- You now know you need to become the master at marketing *you*, because nobody does you like you do you.

- You now know who your audience is and how you can build their trust.

- You now have an endless supply of ideas that you've already curated that you can talk about.

- You now know you need to be consistent because people are unconsciously looking for a reason to not trust you, so you're not going to give them one! You're going to keep showing up. You're going to remain consistent with your message and you're going to be present.

It gets easier

Consistency also breeds confidence. The more you do something, the more confident you become at it, right? So if you've been putting this off because you're not really 'feeling it' yet, it's OK. You've just got to start.

And don't forget what this is leading to. This is the beginning of you being able to create influence.

Influence means that you're able to demonstrate your area of expertise, your thought leadership, your talent and your experience without being all pushy and sales-y. And that means that you're going to be feeling more comfortable with putting out content, because it's not all about the sale. It's about adding value.

So for those of who you who are driven by contribution and service, then guess what? You're going to be doing so much of this it will make you feel amazing about what you're doing literally every single day.

You'll have a voice – and if reshaping your industry is something that is important to you, then you'll be in good stead.

All of this means you're having more impact with your audience.

Which brings us to the *how* we're going to make all of this work.

PART THREE

SHOW ME
THE MONEY

ALL OF THIS THEORY IS GREAT, isn't it? But that's not going to pay the bills!

We need to help you become visible and actually generate a return on investment for the blood, sweat, tears, time, money and energy that you're going to put into becoming visible.

As you know without action, nothing happens and I'm all about getting me (and you!) some results!

It's a bit like thinking 'I want to make a million dollars' so you go to the Googles and you google 'million dollar business plan' (which you can, by the way). You download it. Look at it. Enter your information in. Then put it in a folder and never look at it again.

That million dollars isn't going to make itself!

It's a bit like joining the gym so you can lose weight but you don't actually go.

Without action, nothing changes.

This section is all about strategy and what you need to do to make all of this theory work.

I think we know each other well enough by now for you to know that I am all about the results!

So let's go get them.

7

ACTION JACKSON

DO YOU REMEMBER WHEN you first learned how to drive a car? I remember the first time getting behind the wheel of my parents' car being petrified about all the things I had to think about. The rear-view mirror, side mirror, clutch, brake and accelerator. The indicator. Oops. No, that's the windscreen wiper! The headlights, the lines on the road, the cars, the traffic, the people behind me driving slowly because I was driving slowly. PHEW! It's exhausting just remembering it!

It didn't seem to take long though, after a few lessons, for the feeling of sheer overwhelm and almost paralysing fear to be gone and I started to grow in confidence – and I like to think in ability as well!

This is the same. This is tricky, but it gets better.

Practice, with anything, is key.

Consistency is key.

Yes, it can be painful at first. You'll probably want to have a good cry for a while and throw a tantrum. It's OK. I've got your back. You can do this.

Simply acknowledge that it *may* be a slower learning curve than what you'd like, but you're a freaking rock star and it's important that you nail the rehearsals so you can smash it when you get out on stage.

Return on investment

Getting a return on investment for any time, money and energy that you put into something is important. If you attend a networking event, you want to make sure that you're making connections for referrals and able to get something out of the night as well as give something back. Give and take, right?

Social media and digital marketing is the same. You can't always be just giving, giving, giving all of the time without asking for something in return, otherwise you can end up resenting the people that you've been doing this for, which is totally unhelpful.

But your people aren't going to know what you want them to do unless you spell it out for them. If you're not telling them how to take the steps by making offers or putting together proposals or being very clear about how they can get your help, they'll go and buy from someone else! It's like cooking something beautiful – the smell wafts through the air to their nostrils, but you haven't told them how to purchase it from you, so they go and buy from the store next door!

This is what a call to action is for. Netflix does this all the time. The company gives away a free 15-day 'trial' of its app and then asks you for your money in order to keep using it.

We will need to build up some momentum in order to be able to create this.

Imagine a steam train that has been stopped for 24 hours. It needs a lot fuel to even get moving. You've got to put so much wood into that fire to get it burning so hot so that when you're ready to move, it will go!

Once it does get moving, it moves S L O W L Y. It slowly starts to chug its way along the tracks and eventually reaches a good cruising speed.

But if you stop fuelling it, what happens? It starts to slow down almost straight away and you have to re-stoke that fire to get it moving again. Once again: consistency is key. You need to keep showing up.

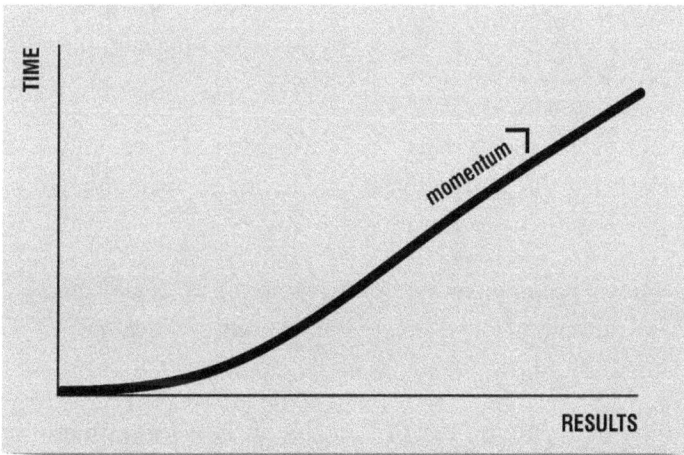

The figure above demonstrates the J curve or the slow burn that it can take before you start seeing results from the non-paid social media posts and digital presence that you're putting up. This brings us to timeframes and when you can expect to see results. It's a great question that I get asked a lot.

I want to be transparent and let you know my timeframes over the past few years:

- I've been building my social media presence since 2010 and have created a Facebook audience of more than 23,000.

  NOTE: I did not do this by buying likes. Buying likes is where you place an advert in the Facebook platform and invite people to 'like your page'. I would not do this.

- I have been blogging and vlogging since 2010. Admittedly, in the early days it wasn't high-quality footage, but the content was ace!

- I have hundreds of videos up on YouTube and Vimeo, and hundreds on Facebook.

- Starting in 2010 it took me 18 months to work out how to leverage all of this work that I was putting into creating content.

- When I started paying for advertising, I was only advertising so I could collect people's names when they registered for a free training of mine.

- I ran live online training webinars twice per week from 2012 through to late 2017. I took six months off running them and restarted these regularly again in 2018.

- I have made more than $4.5 million in sales from using only social media as a way of marketing myself, my blogs and my trainings.

So it's a slow burn, like in the steam train analogy. Each post you put up is like adding another piece of wood to the fire in the engine room of the train. It builds slowly and then becomes a roaring fire. Like the

Pantene advert: 'It won't happen overnight, but it will happen'.

If you wanted to, you could speed up the momentum curve by combining posting on the free platforms (Facebook, LinkedIn, Instagram, etc.) with the paid advertising services that they offer.

Build your own safety net

Most of us actually like being sold to when it's done in such a way that is authentic. Your audience needs to understand the pathway that they're working towards. You need to continue the relationship-building cycle by getting them to take small, baby steps in commitment.

You need to get them into a curated email database so that you can also add value and build relationships outside of social media.

Think about these points:

- What if Facebook goes under tomorrow?
- What if your audience decides to leave Facebook and can't find you again?
- What if LinkedIn bans you?
- What if Instagram is gone?

By taking action to get people onto your email database, you effectively create a safety net for yourself and a way for you to connect with them outside of social media.

But you have to be gracious and continuously add value. Do not send them sales email after sales email trying to sell your stuff. In short, you need to value stack.

Value stacking through your email database

A quick refresher for those of you who may have glazed over for a moment: value stacking is where you keep adding more and more value into the marketplace in the form of free content, which is either 'opt-in' or available to all.

So now let's look at ways that you can value stack on both your social media channels and your email database.

Value stacking is all about building micro-commitments with your people. The more they interact, the more likely it will be that they continue to interact. Once they're on your email database, do not just send them a newsletter that has no substance or value in it. That is lame. Disrespectful. And drop-dead boring.

With that out of the way, we can progress!

Now that they're on your email database, you can share:

- Your latest blog
- Your whitepaper (a problem-solving guide)
- Anything else you want to send them, which we'll go through in a moment.

But what then? They need to take action.

So you could offer them:

- A course
- A conversation with you
- A presentation

- An in-person visit
- A book

or …

- You could ask them to BUY something from you. Gasp!

They just need to see what that next step looks like, otherwise they don't know what that next step is!

I have found for myself and for my clients, 70% of sales come from people who have been on an email list because they've 'opted in' for something – for example a webinar or a free guide. Not bad, huh? Even if you're building a side hustle while working or parenting, that's a good statistic to know!

How this works

For every piece of value you share, you get one 'value stacking point'.

It's like a fun game, right?

- Send them a blog, and you get one value stacking point
- Send them the link to your latest article and you get another value. stacking point
- Send them your whitepaper and you get another value stacking point
- Send them a link to your latest video and you get another value stacking point

Now you have four value stacking points in the 'bank'.
When you have five value stacking points, you have earned the right to ask them to take some kind of action. You don't *have* to

ask for something at number five, but why wouldn't you? It could be to sign up for a webinar, opt-in for your latest course, buy your book or something else that gets them to commit with either their information or their money.

Other ideas of things to share that would add value are:

- Solving a problem through email
- Sharing a video
- Sharing something you found that would help them
- Sharing something that helped you when you were down/demotivated

The most awesome thing about all of this is that you can duplicate it on social media! You literally replicate the value stacking process over on your social media channels.

Putting it into action

I recommend sending an email through your database twice per week at least. You can increase this to more often if you have more value to add. Just make sure that it's adding value and that it's solving problems or helping in some way.

Nobody wants to contribute to the spam epidemic; however, it's imperative that your audience is receiving emails from you regularly so that they remember who you are.

Before you get worried that they're going to be annoyed with you, it's OK. They'll have the option to unsubscribe if they feel like you're not doing the right thing. If they start to complain because you're adding value to them, inspiring them and helping them, then they were probably never going to be your client anyway.

Many people won't open the emails that you send when you send them – don't be surprised if many people play 'catch up' with their emails over the weekend.

Focus on the audience and helping them and you'll be OK.

Value stacking through social media

On social media, a micro-commitment is a click, a like, a comment, and even better, opting-in for one of your free resources so you can add them to your database.

The way to value stack through social media is by posting a photo, some text or a video. Just like value stacking through email, you get one value stacking point for every piece of value you share through social media.

How can you add value on social media? You could:

- Share a link to your latest blog, article or video
- Give them a way for them to download a tool that you might have created that would help them
- Solve a problem through your posts
- Inspire them
- Share a photo of you helping the people you work with
- Share a photo of your lifestyle (walking, your kids if you want to share that online, your dogs and even your favourite coffee)
- Share something you found that would help them
- Share something that helped you when you were down/demotivated

Any of these will earn you one value stacking point. And you know what happens when you get to five points right? Yes! You have earned the right to ask them to take some kind of action.

Putting it into action

What I'd recommend you do on social media is to post ideally a few times per day. For those of you starting out, start with once per day.

The rotation of value-stacking posts could go as follows:

1. Inspiring text-based post. You could tell a story or share some words of inspiration

2. A professional photo of you combined with some text in a post

3. A video that you have found in your travels that matches your message and helps your audience

4. A photo of you working with your people or doing the work that you love to do (showing you in action)

5. A live video or a pre-recorded video of you would be excellent.

You'll repeat this (ideally a few times per day) or at least once per day.

- Monday is a text post
- Tuesday is a photo post
- Wednesday is a video
- And so on

This creates a great catalogue of content on social media for your audience to get to know, learn to like and trust you and additionally, your audience can see that you are present and that you are paying attention to your page.

You've done it!

The payoff to all of this is that you're not just shouting, contributing to the white noise that is propagated online. You're actually putting valuable content out into the world that is useful and helpful.

Your audience is going to love the heck out of you, because finally someone is coming into their world who is willing to show up and be themselves and, in turn, give them permission to be the best version of themselves that they, too, can be.

This is called leadership and it's going to help you grow your tribe of loyal followers who listen to you and take on what you have to say. This in turn ensures that you are creating a message-to-market match.

Implementing this strategy will form a solid foundation that will withstand the test of time. It doesn't matter where you market yourself, how the platforms change, what new ones come into place or what platforms disappear, this is a marketing strategy that is timeless.

The other beautiful thing about this process is that you can actually measure the result of what you've been doing.

For example, if you get one new consultation request after three weeks (which may have taken you 15 value stacking points to achieve) then you can replicate that, or you can increase the timeframe in which you accumulate those value-stacking points and get that next consultation faster.

And you know what that means, right? Return on investment for all the effort you're putting in. What's not to love?

Express review

It has to be you. No one does you better than you, and only you can build the relationship you need with your audience.

Perfection is a myth. You don't have to show up online like you have it all together all of the time.

You're the boss. Treat the entire digital world like it's your 'OWN' network.

Once you discover your zone of awesomeness you'll have endless content ideas.

You need to know who your audience is.

People need to be able to find you easily if they're wanting to follow up on something that you've said or shared.

Pick your platforms strategically and know where you need to invest the time to start. Once you have a solid foundation, you can then start learning and posting on the next one. And then the next one. And so it snowballs.

It takes time to build momentum.

If you want to generate larger volumes of leads (names and email addresses) in a shorter amount of time you could 'pay to play'. Pay to play means paying for a placement in newsfeeds of your target audience. It's kind of like placing an advert in a newspaper in the old days!

Value stacking matrix

PLATFORM	VALUE PIECE 1	VALUE PIECE 2	VALUE PIECE 3	VALUE PIECE 4	VALUE PIECE 5	CALL TO ACTION	REPEAT
FACEBOOK							
YOUR WEBSITE							
LINKEDIN							
INSTAGRAM							
VLOGGING							
EMAIL LIST							
PODCAST							
FACEBOOK LIVE							
IGTV							
TWITTER							

CONCLUSION

I remember sitting in my tiny office (more like a storage room) in my old house when I started playing with and testing social media marketing and advertising.

I had three kids under the age of eight and my husband was practically not home for six months of the year while he was managing his family's farm during grape season.

It was tough. I didn't know what I was doing. I didn't know how to make it work, I just knew that somehow I would be able to get this thing off the ground and use my knowledge to help people all around the world.

I would start work before dropping the children off at school or day care and often had my son home with me a few days a week. I remember one time when I was working, I told my son I just needed five more minutes, but when I came out of my office I found an entire packet of biscuits had been eaten behind the couch because my 'five more minutes' had turned into more than an hour. #motherguilt

I'd rush to get the children, come home, and keep working. I'd quickly make dinner, throw it down all of our throats, spend some time with the kids, put them to bed and get back to work.

Most nights I'd finish up around midnight, to go to bed to a snoring husband with my brain wired and not able to sleep. I kept this up for about 18 months and it nearly killed me.

On top of all of that, I live in the middle of nowhere in country Victoria without a peer network to keep me on track. My friends were great. My husband was supportive. But I really lacked people who 'got me' and who could steer me in the right direction.

If I can create what I have from here, then you can do it from anywhere.

Social media is getting noisier and noisier and your audience isn't going to tolerate a half-arsed attempt at building a profile. Honestly, they'll just tune out and find someone else to listen to, which is devastating, because you are awesome and you deserve to be seen and heard.

It's got to be you, particularly because so many other people in your industry are too afraid to show up! They're worried about the judgement of others, how they're going to look and what people are going to say about them, and they buy into that fear of not being good enough.

You're better than that and you've learned that you are an expert at what you do. You've got the evidence to support that!

As I've shown you, it's critically important now – and will only become more so as time goes on – that you are showing up online and talking to your audience in a way that they understand and can hear you.

As for the time that it takes, yes, it's going to take a time commitment from you. However, I trust that you've seen how you can use essentially one piece of content in multiple places. You've seen how an investment of your time will pay off if you choose to follow the strategy that I've mapped out for you.

The added benefit to all of this is that you'll have a way of being able to sell – without being sales-y, pushy or feeling like all you're doing is hawking your wares.

And that means you'll get a return on investment. Cha-ching!

WHERE TO FROM HERE?

There are few things that I recommend you do:

1. Complete all of the activities in this book if you haven't already. You can download activity sheets at www.nicolamoras.com.au/visible

2. Take one step forward every single day and celebrate that you have done that.

3. If you want more help with this, head over to any of my profiles or my website and let's connect. I promise I won't give you some canned autobot response!

ACKNOWLEDGEMENTS

There are so many people to thank and pay homage to, because it really does take a whole team of people – a tribe if you will – to bring something like this to life. Without my team, this book wouldn't be here.

To my family first and foremost for your undying belief in what I do and me. Thank you.

To Kelly Irving, who helped me right from the word go, taking this from an idea to a plan to bringing this to life. Your insights into how to make this a book of substance versus a piece of fluff that nobody would understand nor implement were solid gold. Thank you for setting me up from the start for success.

To my editor, Lu Sexton, for your insights and being gentle with me and not allowing me to buy into my doubts that this was ever going to make it to print!

To one of my very best friends, Jo Muirhead, for reminding me of how much I know and for always being there no matter what to inspire, guide and kick me in the ass to get me out of my own way and just keep writing!

To my mentors over the years for your support and encouragement to keep going.

Thanks also need to go to Chris Howard for doing something so unusual in this industry – writing my foreword without asking for anything in return. For your kind words and generosity towards someone you don't know very well, thank you.

To Janine Garner, my mentor while writing this book, for your constant reminders about why this book is important and that I know more than I think I know. Thank you for really seeing me and holding me to a higher standard.

To my parents, Karl and Jacqueline, thank you for showing me by example how to chase your dreams, to pick yourself up after a perceived failure and keep going. If there is such a thing as a resilience gene, I thank you both for passing it on to me. For your unwavering support and for seeing me for who I am, thank you.

To my children, Tiana, Ezrie and Jake. Thank you for reminding me the importance of having fun. For teaching me on a daily basis how to be a better human. Most of all, thank you for allowing me to share with you what I see as your pure potential as humans who are going to get out there and change the world. Thanks for choosing me to be your mum. I love you.

And to my husband, Dom. Thank you for choosing me every single day, even when I probably don't deserve to be chosen. You have supported every single hare-brained scheme I cook up and I have no doubt that you have had numerous doubts that most of the time you don't share with me: you just say 'You've got this,' or 'It will be OK'. Thank you for listening to my downloads, my debriefing, my ah-ha's, my ramblings and my insights, for it allows me to process my thoughts – annoying as that is for you because there's always a story, right? Without you by my side, I wouldn't be doing my life's work.

Finally, thank you to YOU for reading this and for taking what you can from it to help you to reach the people that you want to help. I appreciate you.

www.ingramcontent.com/pod-product-compliance
Lightning Source LLC
Chambersburg PA
CBHW031940190326
41519CB00007B/595